Healing Rest

Healing Rest

AN INVITATION FOR *Mommas* WHO
CARRY SO MUCH TO LEAN INTO THE
ARMS OF THE *One* WHO HOLDS IT *All*

BECKY THOMPSON

W PUBLISHING GROUP

AN IMPRINT OF THOMAS NELSON

Published in Nashville, Tennessee, by W Publishing, an imprint of Thomas Nelson. W Publishing and Thomas Nelson are registered trademarks of HarperCollins Christian Publishing, Inc.

Thomas Nelson titles may be purchased in bulk for educational, business, fund-raising, or sales promotional use. For information, please e-mail SpecialMarkets@ThomasNelson.com.

The author is represented by Alive Literary Agency, www.aliveliterary.com.

Unless otherwise noted, Scripture quotations are taken from the Holy Bible, New International Version®, NIV®. Copyright © 1973, 1978, 1984, 2011 by Biblica, Inc.® Used by permission of Zondervan. All rights reserved worldwide. www.zondervan.com. The "NIV" and "New International Version" are trademarks registered in the United States Patent and Trademark Office by Biblica, Inc.® Quotations marked CSB are taken from the Christian Standard Bible®. Copyright © 2017 by Holman Bible Publishers. Used by permission. Christian Standard Bible® and CSB® are federally registered trademarks of Holman Bible Publishers. Quotations marked ESV are taken from the ESV® Bible (The Holy Bible, English Standard Version®). Copyright © 2001 by Crossway, a publishing ministry of Good News Publishers. Used by permission. All rights reserved. Quotations marked KJV are taken from the King James Version. Public domain. Quotations marked NKJV are taken from the New King James Version®. Copyright © 1982 by Thomas Nelson. Used by permission. All rights reserved. Quotations marked NLT are taken from the Holy Bible, New Living Translation. Copyright © 1996, 2004, 2015 by Tyndale House Foundation. Used by permission of Tyndale House Ministries, Carol Stream, Illinois 60188. All rights reserved.

Italics added to direct Scripture quotations are the author's emphasis.

This book is not intended to replace the advice of a trained psychological or medical professional.

Portions of this book have been adapted from previous works by Becky Thompson.

Any internet addresses, phone numbers, or company or product information printed in this book are offered as a resource and are not intended in any way to be or to imply an endorsement by Thomas Nelson, nor does Thomas Nelson vouch for the existence, content, or services of these sites, phone numbers, companies, or products beyond the life of this book.

ISBN 978-0-7852-4444-8 (softcover)
ISBN 978-0-7852-4395-3 (eBook)
ISBN 978-0-7852-4446-2 (audiobook)

Library of Congress Control Number: 2024944747

Printed in the United States of America

24 25 26 27 28 LBC 5 4 3 2 1

CONTENTS

Introduction   vii

Chapter 1: When Life Feels Like a Lot   1

Chapter 2: When You Know the World Isn't Safe   21

Chapter 3: When You Just Want to Hide   41

Chapter 4: When All the Alarms Are Sounding   61

Chapter 5: When Your Soul Needs Rest   81

Chapter 6: When Your Body Needs Rest   101

Chapter 7: When Your Mind Needs Rest   119

Chapter 8: When You Need Calming Connection   137

Chapter 9: When You Start to Heal   159

Acknowledgments   179

Notes   181

About the Author   185

Introduction

TO YOU, MOMMA, BEFORE WE BEGIN

(Start Here!)

BEFORE YOU HELD THIS BOOK IN YOUR HANDS, THE LORD SAW YOU AND KNEW you needed rest. Before you listened to this audiobook or your eyes skimmed across the screen of your phone or tablet . . . before these words were presented to you in whatever way they have come to you, the Lord saw this exact moment. He knew what would be happening in your day, the stresses you'd face this week, and the situations that would weigh the heaviest on your heart during this season of your life. He knew you would need Him right here . . . right now.

And in His kindness, He orchestrated all the steps behind the scenes for the last few years, leading you to this one so He could make sure you were reminded of this very important truth on this very specific day:

You are safely held by a good God who loves you.

Those words need a little space to breathe. Don't rush past them. Look at them again.

Now, here's the thing. Maybe those words aren't new to you. Maybe you *know* that God is good and that He is near and that He is holding you safely in His arms. You've read it in your Bible. You've heard it from trusted pastors and Bible study teachers. You've lived out the reality of these words day after day for as long as you have known Jesus. Perhaps you've even spoken similar words when encouraging others.

But I wonder . . . Do you *feel* safely held right now?.

Perhaps, my friend, you're in a part of your story where you need to be reminded that all those things you once so easily believed about God are *still* true today: He *still* is with you. He *still* cares about the things that are breaking your heart. And despite the way life is unfolding around you right now, He *still* has everything under control.

I have a sense that you need someone to point to the truth you already know and say it in a way that helps you remember what it feels like to *be* secure once again.

Or maybe . . . maybe the idea of being safely held by a good God is new to you. Maybe you want those words to be true. You wonder what it would mean if they were true. And you're reading these words because more than anything you, too, want to *feel* safely held. Because maybe then you could actually rest.

Deep breath.

You aren't the only one. I don't know all the details of what is taking place in your life right now, but I have a pretty good idea of what is going on in your heart. I have a hunch that we are probably a lot alike. Maybe not when it comes to the ages of our kids or how we put food on the table for our families or how we spend our time. Maybe not in the stories we have lived or how long we have been alive or whether we are married. But I have a feeling we are similar when it comes to the important stuff. We both want peace, security, and rest, but we feel pressured to worry, hold everything together, and rush.

Listen, I'm not a stranger to the need for peace. I understand how hard—impossible—it can be to find rest. I've been chronically overwhelmed by the world around me and the swirl of my own thoughts within me since I was young. Some of my earliest memories are of my fears and how I dealt with them. I understand anxiety, exhaustion, and stress.

I also know what it means to live with daily access to Jesus through the power of the Holy Spirit inside me. I hear God's voice. I follow His Word. I know His presence. I've felt His love. I've seen miracles with my own eyes. I've sensed Him miraculously shift my heart and emotions. He's realigned my thinking. He's straightened the path before me. He's walked with me daily. He is good. He is kind. And He holds me safely in His arms.

But most days? Most days I'm intensely aware of my need for Him because I'm a woman who loves Jesus and also happens to live with a dysregulated nervous system (words I have learned only in the last few years but still don't entirely understand because I'm not a doctor or health professional). We'll talk more about the nervous system and how it impacts our lives later, but basically, I'm saying that I'm a woman who loves Jesus and has lived through some stuff that has shifted the way my mind, heart, and body live in this broken world.

I guess that's a long way of saying I'm a bit of a mess, and I need Jesus as much as you do.

I'm not a woman you'd take tips from when it comes to organization or rhythms or planning. I'm not the friend you call when you forget what time the open house takes place at the grade school or when you're having an issue with your teenager and want advice. (I'm just trying to figure it out on my own over here.) But I can absolutely fill the role in your life of Jesus-lovin', Holy Ghost–prayin', often-stressy-messy-bestie (who occasionally won't text you back for three to five business days if I feel too overwhelmed to reply).

I get it. I understand what it feels like when you're so busy, burned-out, or anxious that God feels far, even though you *know* He is close.

In 2019 (prepandemic, mind you), I wrote a book about anxiety and my journey out of the forest of fear. The Lord had given me a vision of a woman standing in the woods at night, blindfolded. It seemed as if she had been kidnapped, driven to the middle of nowhere, and dropped off. She didn't know how to find her way forward. She didn't know how to get out of the woods. There was no sign of which way to go, so in her desperation she cried out, "Helloooo!" She waited, listening and watching, but no one came for her. In that moment, the Lord spoke to my heart and said, *You're going back for her so we can lead her out together.*[1]

And we did. Writing that book called *Peace* and teaching from it for years has changed my life. I am even more confident of God's promise to lead His daughters toward the Son, who is the Prince of Peace. I am even more grateful for the healing that comes in so many ways because of Jesus's sacrifice. And I am even more aware that I'm not alone. After leading tens of thousands of women through the book and online studies, I understand so many women are also in the forest, each wondering if she's the only one who can't find her way to the clearing.

But the forest of fear is not the only forest a Christian woman may find herself in without warning, wondering how she may return to safety, peace, and rest. So I wonder: What forest are you walking through? What dimly lit, uncertain, or unexpected path do you find yourself walking on right now? Are you in the forest of some surprise season you didn't anticipate? Are you walking through the forest of exhaustion? Grief? Confusion? Loss? Betrayal? Transition?

Have you walked the forest of divorce or sickness or something that has blindsided you? Is this season of motherhood or life in general its own forest? Or, friend, perhaps you have lived in many of these connected woods. I wonder if you relate to the woman in my vision who found herself unexpectedly feeling her way forward in the dark, overwhelmed by uncertainty. I relate to her because I have been her. I know what it feels like to wonder if life will always be the way it is right now. To wonder if I will ever find blue skies and space to breathe on this journey, where the light has seemed so dim. I know that craving for rest in a life that won't slow down, and I must keep pressing forward.

I have lived in the forest. And I have lived in the clearing. And I have learned that the God who doesn't change meets us in both places, offering hope and healing for our hearts, minds, and bodies.

The God we see and hear more clearly when the fear lifts, the overwhelm subsides, the uncertainty ends, and the heartache heals is the very same God who holds us safely as we journey through whatever forest we face. Even in those places, the ones where we're convinced we are all alone, He is there. He holds you because that is who He is. He is the God who holds His children.

I have teenagers now, but I remember when I had three little-bitty kids I held all the time. It seems like all I did was comfort and carry and rock all day and often all night. I remember one night in particular when my daughter's voice came through her little brother's baby monitor down the hall from her own room. Sometimes she'd sleep talk or even cry. I got to her room as quickly as I could to keep her from waking anyone else, climbed into her little twin-sized bed, and held her against me. "I'll hold you," I whispered as she leaned into me, relaxed, and fell back asleep.

I kissed her forehead and slipped into the hall just as her baby brother cried out in the dark from his room. I found him standing at the edge of his crib, tears already pouring down his sleepy cheeks. I pulled him into my arms, and we settled into the nearby chair.

"I'll hold you," I whispered as I hushed him and rocked him back and forth. "Momma will hold you."

In every stage of motherhood, our arms hold so much, and often our hearts hold even more. But in the middle of that night, as I rocked my son back to sleep, I heard the Lord softly whisper to me, *Becky, I'll hold you.* These are the same words He has told me in every season since.

My friend, in this moment, I deeply believe you are reading this page because God is speaking the same words to you. He calls you by name and says, *I will hold you.* He will hold you when life has been a lot and the world feels unsafe. He will hold you when you want to hide and when all the alarms in your mind and body are sounding. He will hold you close and give you rest for your soul, strength for your body, and peace for your mind. He will hold you when you feel discouraged or disconnected and need His calming comfort. He will hold you as you heal.

Come join me as we encounter the God who promises peace, the same God who offers rest, the Lord who made a way to be with us so we don't ever have to carry life's heavy load alone or afraid.

Take one more deep breath, and let's pray together as we lean into Jesus and find healing rest.

Father, may the momma reading these words right now experience peace in Your presence. As she reads the pages ahead, may she find security in the safety of Your love. Please lift the heaviness. It has been too much to bear. May the effects of exhaustion, stress, and overwhelm melt like wax as You hold her close. May the revelation of Your love bring healing rest to every area of her heart, mind, and body. She can trust You to hold it all. Help her believe it. I ask in Jesus's name, amen.

Chapter 1

WHEN LIFE FEELS LIKE A LOT

Hope for the Stressed-Out Momma
Who Hasn't Stopped to Heal

I STOOD AT THE FRONT OF A ROOM FILLED WITH WOMEN WHO DESPERATELY needed peace and rest, and I was one of them. I had flown in to speak at a conference, sharing a message that would help mommas find hope and healing for their anxious and exhausted hearts. I had scriptures and stories and important points I prayerfully planned to present. I'd describe some of the funniest moments from my own journey and hope they'd laugh along with me. (I think sometimes women, mommas especially, just need to laugh at how ridiculous life can be.) It was going to be a good day. The only problem was, I felt a little like a fraud.

The event's host introduced me to the audience. With a smile, I walked up the stairs to the platform, tired not just from traveling across the country but also from all the life I've traveled over the last few decades. I wondered if anyone noticed. I've gotten pretty skilled at masking how I really feel. I had chatted with women before the event began. I had smiled and prayed and laughed during the preservice meeting. I had raised my hands in worship. Outwardly, I looked the part of a Christian woman who could deliver a message on rest. Inwardly, well . . . Inwardly, I just wanted a nap and a break and, honestly, for the pressures of daily life to relent a bit.

I placed my iPad on the podium and scrolled to the top of my notes. Bold capital letters spelled out the word *PEACE*, and underneath it I had written these words:

The Lord wants to meet with you, encourage you, and fill you with fresh hope and His perfect peace. This refreshment isn't just for you. It is for your family.

What I had written was true. But I wondered: How was I supposed to bring a message of hope and healing when my own heart felt so unbearably heavy? How was I supposed to share that God wants to refresh our hearts when rest seemed so far out of my own reach? These moms had left their families and slipped away for a few hours to refill their own cups. They needed exactly what the Lord had sent me to offer them. I just needed it too.

I thanked the host for her kind introduction, and I scanned the room, wondering how many of the women in front of me felt the same way I did. How many of them were smiling back at me while hiding their own exhaustion too? I met their eyes with my own. Without them saying a word, I knew their hearts were asking: *What are you going to tell me that can actually help me rest? What are you going to say that can bring security to my life? Just tell me what to do to have peace, and I'll do it.*

Some of them held paper and pens, waiting for the wisdom they trusted I'd share. Maybe they believed that if I could give them the right steps, they could follow a procedure to find peace. Some of us love checklists, don't we? Like many mommas, maybe you love to write things down and check them off and see the progress you've made because so many of your to-dos are invisible. It's like there's a running mental list no one can see but you. You take care of so many things that go unnoticed by everyone else . . . all the little details that are quickly undone or consumed or need to be done again tomorrow because they're part of a cycle. So some mommas keep lists and keep organized. (I say "some" because I'm not one of them.)

Are you? Do you love to write out your to-do list with coordinating colors in a pretty planner? I love that for you. Listen, I love list-making supplies. Yes, the supplies. I love aesthetic pens and highlighters and stickers and matching sticky notes and paper clips. I love the way they look, but they have never helped me stay organized.

I used to think that if I had the *right* tools, I'd finally become the most detailed momma. So for a long time I'd buy different planners at the start of every year, thinking they were the answer to my overwhelm. But they weren't. They didn't help me sort through the clutter in my heart. I only ever made it a few weeks into using them before getting distracted. As it turns out, the imperfect planner was not the problem.

My system of organization is far more . . . *organic? Artistic?* Okay, it's *chaotic.* My desk is full of doctors' appointment reminders and bill-pay confirmation numbers scribbled onto weird little scraps of paper or the back of an envelope I found on the kitchen counter or in my car. My heart and mind seem to match my desk.

The truth is, I'm a messy, neurodivergent mom who intensely loves Jesus, and I'm not the best at making or keeping lists. I'm not the best at order or procedure. My mind is distractible, jumping from one thing to the next. For most of my life I have been a chronic rusher and perpetual worrier. I definitely don't sound like the sort of woman who could write a book called *Healing Rest.* Trust me, Jesus and I have had plenty of conversations about all the women I think are far more qualified to write these words.

But here's the thing. I write from a place of understanding

what it feels like to be in the thick of it and trust that the Lord meets us right here. That's the message of most of my work.

Over the course of the last ten years, I have shared many stories about the ways God has met me in my life, my motherhood, and my marriage. Stories about following God and trusting Him have filled websites and book pages, radio programs and podcasts. I have been in every way an open book (yep, I agree that's cheesy), praying that women just like you would find peace, hope, and healing as I point to God's Word and His Spirit, who is always with us. But here's my little secret: I have never written a book that I haven't needed myself.

I needed "Grace-Filled Truth for the Momma's Heart" in my book *Hope Unfolding*. And I needed to rediscover my "Marriage in the Midst of Motherhood" in *Love Unending*. I needed to stand on *Truth Unchanging*. I needed to remember I serve a *God So Close*, and I desperately needed *Peace: Hope and Healing for the Anxious Momma's Heart*.

My mom and I wrote *Tonight We Pray for the Momma* and the *Midnight Mom Devotional*, and we run an online ministry for over two million moms, praying for them nightly as they go through all their midnight moments of motherhood. My mom and I often say that we can pray mommas through some of their hardest and heaviest seasons because we have lived them. We *are* the midnight moms we are praying for many nights.

So I suppose I shouldn't have been surprised when the Lord told me I was to offer a message of healing rest for the mommas at that conference, telling them they can experience peace because they're safely held by a good God who loves them. Since I had lived all the messages I had put into books and shared from stages so far, this would be no different. I certainly needed rest. I was exhausted to my core and carried only by the grace of God and the presence of the Holy Spirit. I needed Jesus to lift the heaviness and heal my overwhelmed heart more than anything. Life had been a lot lately. And I knew it had been for every woman in the room that day too.

I looked down at my notes. I didn't have any lists, steps, or to-dos for those moms to copy into their notebooks and check off once accomplished, which would lift their burden of exhaustion. I didn't have a strategy that had previously worked for me, tried and true, which, if they followed, could help them experience deep rest too. All I had to share with them was an invitation to meet with Jesus and let His love bring healing to every endlessly exhausted heart.

So that's exactly what I offered.

For the rest of that conference, I spoke the truth we *all* needed to hear. I told those ladies that I was tired to my bones and that I needed the Lord just as much as they did. I pointed to the scriptures we could all stand on, and I offered assurance that the Lord brings peace and He is near.

So many hearts began to heal that day . . . my own included. It wasn't until I got home and sat at my desk, thinking back over the weekend, that I heard the Lord speak so kindly: *Becky, you're not a fraud. You're a friend.*

A fraud makes empty promises and pretends to be something they aren't. A friend reaches out and says, "I understand because I feel the same way too." As C. S. Lewis stated in his book *The Four Loves*, "Friendship . . . is born at the moment when one man says to another 'What! You too? I thought that no one but myself . . .'"[1] And that is why throughout this book and in every other, I call you *friend*. The Lord has given me the sweetest gift of standing on the path of motherhood, meeting women right in the middle of their journeys, and asking if they'd allow me to walk with them for a while.

I am not the mom who stands on the other side shouting, "You'll make it!" I'm the mom who says, "I thought I might find you here. We'll get through this together because we have the Holy Spirit as our guide. Let's follow Him out of this forest. The One who leads us, loves us."

So, my friend, whether we are meeting for the first time or have raised our children together, I want to start by saying . . . I thought I might find you here. I believe the Lord sent me to meet you because He understands just how much you need rest.

OF COURSE YOU NEED REST

I know your journey has been long. I bet you're so tired. I bet that pack you've been carrying is so heavy. I can't take the responsibilities you've been shouldering, but I can help you pass the deeply pressing burden of it all to Jesus. I can help you remember who you are in Him and where He is with you. He's right there . . . and right here, offering us both rest.

That's what you're hoping to discover here, isn't it? Safety. Peace. Rest. You're hoping to find security in a world where life seems to shift beneath your feet because, if you're being honest, nothing feels secure right now. Your people, the ones you love most, don't really seem safe or settled either. I have a feeling you wouldn't be reading this if you, or if they, did.

The weight of worrying about everyone and everything can be overwhelming, can't it? The mental load of motherhood in every season can be too much at times (or all the time). The constant rush and relentless work are the *most*. You just want a break. I get it. Me too.

The last few years have been a lot, haven't they? In your home. In your community. In the world. When the world fell apart back in 2020, we did the best we could to soldier through, putting one foot in front of the other. We made the best choices we could. We kept ourselves and our families as safe as we could. We figured it out. But it was exhausting. It was painful. There was so much loss—the loss of loved ones, the loss of jobs, the loss of security or the life you thought you'd have . . . the loss of peace. And maybe you haven't fully processed all you experienced. Maybe you're reading this book the year it releases, or maybe it is a decade later and your heart still carries the pain from that past season (or some other painful past).

Maybe you see a counselor or a therapist. Maybe you've found ways to cope or strategies that bring relief when you're feeling overwhelmed or spiraling in a swirl of stress. But maybe you *still* don't feel settled. Some events in our lives just mark us that way. They change the way we see ourselves and the world and our place in it.

Perhaps it wasn't the pandemic that made you feel unsafe or unsettled. Maybe it was something that took place before or perhaps after. But I wonder, Does it ever feel as if you woke up in the middle of the night to a world full of chaos and confusion, and your heart hasn't been able to relax back into feeling safe enough to really rest? Does it feel like there's no time to stop and heal?

My friend, we experienced all this uncertainty over the last few years while also going through the hard and heavy that happens in life even when there isn't global unrest. We have continued to endure a national and worldwide crisis and *still* have the pressures and pain of life—perhaps an unexpected diagnosis to understand, a miscarriage to mourn, a marriage in trouble, aging parents to care for, loved ones who passed from cancer or chronic disease, terror in our schools, estrangement in our families, and other blindsiding events. We had family issues or money issues or school issues or health issues or job issues or . . . you name it. Real life doesn't stop because the rest of the world falls apart around us. I suppose it never does.

There's no reason to wonder why your heart needs healing.

There's a clear need for you to find rest. Of course you need peace. Your heart likely craves security. You have journeyed a long road that has brought you to this moment.

Even now, I have a feeling that your body feels tense and you're reading this with shallow breaths. Maybe? Let's do something together. Take a moment with me and unclench your jaw. Let your shoulders drop. Relax your forehead. Take a deep breath. Breathe in all the air you need. Blow out all you've been holding in . . . Good. Maybe do that one more time.

You're safe.

Really. Even now. Even with all you've been through. Even with all they're talking about on the news this week. Even with the current state of the world. Even with all the things that are popping into your head at this exact moment. Even when the fears are so loud, they seem to be shrieking: *But you're not safe!*

Peace.

Even here . . . even now . . . you're safely held by a good God who loves you and promises to never leave you. That's one thing of which I am certain. And just as I stood at the front of that conference and invited those women to discover healing rest in Jesus, I offer the same invitation to you now, as you read these words.

If you could see with your spiritual eyes in this exact moment, if you could blink a few times and suddenly everything in the unseen world around you could become perfectly visible, you'd find that the Lord is close—not just the idea of

Him, but the Lord Himself is with you. His arms are wrapped securely around you. His face is turned toward you. If you could look up into His gaze, you'd see the love in His eyes— eyes that are full of compassion and fiery authority, eyes fully fixed on you, eyes fully aware of your situation and fully perceiving all parts of your story. You'd find that He has everything you need in this exact moment and everything you'll need for all the moments ahead.

Deep breath.

If you could hear perfectly with your spiritual ears in this exact moment, if you could tune out the sounds around you and the roaring din of your own internal thoughts, fears, and plans, you'd hear the Lord's heartbeat and discover that it is beating so close to your own. You'd hear Him speak softly and powerfully,

I have you. I didn't let you go. You're not alone. I know that sometimes you wonder if you will ever feel peace. I know what you've tried. I've caught all the tears you've cried, and I have held you through it all. It's not up to you to find your way forward through this season on your own. Listen to My heartbeat. Hear the peace in My voice. I have overcome everything you're going to face, and we will walk through the days ahead together. I love you, and I won't leave you. Rest in Me.

Deep breath.

My friend, you are not now, nor have you ever been since the day you came to believe in Jesus as the Son of God, alone in your long walk home. You do not have to keep doing it all in your own strength, feeling burned-out, broken down, or breathless. Jesus has peace for you, and you can experience the peace found in His presence in two specific ways.

Peace comes when we see that there is a way forward. It's as if we are able to pull future relief into the present moment. Hope springs to life in our hearts when we imagine what it may look like when we reach the other side of where we stand today. We may have peace in knowing the One called the Prince of Peace will lead us through it.

But I believe we can also experience the peace Jesus offers right in the middle of the hard and heavy. We don't have to wait until we reach the other side of the struggle because the Prince of Peace holds us safely even while we stand in the midst of uncertainty.

HELD BY LOVE

Throughout Scripture, we see evidence of God's desire to hold His children securely in a world that is anything but safe.

In Exodus, we read the story about a baby boy named Moses who grew to become the deliverer of the Israelites, God's chosen people. He was born during a time when the king of Egypt feared God's people, who were living as slaves in his kingdom. This king was concerned God's people would fight against him and win because they were so numerous. So Pharaoh decreed that all baby boys would be put to death.

Pharaoh may have been afraid of God's people, but Moses's momma, Jochebed, feared the Lord. She hid her baby boy for three months, stifling his cries, concealing his very existence, likely praying and trusting God for her son's safety daily. Exodus 2:3 tells us that when she saw she could hide him no more, she still didn't give up. She waterproofed a small basket and put her baby inside.

I've heard this story since I was a young girl, and sometimes the reality of what Jochebed did seems like a tale from long ago in a land far away. The truth is that a mother, just like you or me, put her tiny infant in a basket and put that basket in the river.

Can you imagine your own child, at only three months old, blinking into the bright sun as he lies helplessly in a handmade boat at the edge of the water? Can you imagine how intensely you'd want to pull him to your chest, wrap your arms tightly around him, and keep him safe? I can't imagine the pain or fear or anguish in Jochebed's heart as she let go. I cannot fathom the ache of slipping away, hand over my mouth, trying not to draw attention, stifling my own sobs while silently pleading with the Lord to spare my baby's life.

I can't imagine what Jochebed experienced that day, but I do know what it feels like to trust the Lord with my children and plead with Him on their behalf. I do know what it feels like to have done all I can in a trying situation and realize that I must release it to Jesus. I do know the ache of a momma who wishes her love was enough to keep her children safe.

Just as Moses's momma was not just trusting her own waterproofing work to keep her baby secure, neither do we trust only our own efforts to uphold our families. Just as Jochebed was trusting the Lord to carry Moses, we can trust the Lord to care for our kids. In a situation far from safe, we can trust that even when we can't hold our babies securely with our love, they will be safely held by God.

Moses was pulled from the water by Pharaoh's daughter and grew up in the palace as a prince of Egypt. The Lord led Moses throughout his life and used him to set God's people free from bondage. Surely the Lord carried him safely on the water, but the Lord's hand to uphold Moses was evident in Moses's life beyond the small basket boat, because that is what God does. We have a God who upholds.

Can I remind you of something? The Lord has you. *Really.* He knows the water from which you will be pulled. He also knows that you've been trusting your own waterproofing to keep yourself and your family afloat. You've been doing all you know to do to keep yourself and those you love from sinking.

I know the world feels unsafe. I know pain is real, and the problems of life keep coming, and your heart may feel heavy because you're stressed out, anxious, and tired. That tight grip you've held, doing your best to protect everyone and everything, is so exhausting. Isn't it? It's hard work holding your whole world in your own hands.

Momma, here is some heart-healing truth as we begin. The Lord is close, and while the situations you're facing may feel far from safe, you are safely held by arms that were once spread out on a cross so they could wrap you up for all eternity. That's your present position. In this very moment, you are held by the arms of Love.

Can you close your eyes for a moment and imagine what it might feel like to rest in His arms? Imagine how your tension would release; the pressure that makes you feel as if you should rush or worry would ease; and your thoughts would still like a stormy sea going suddenly silent. Really pause to picture it. What would it feel like to be held by Jesus?

I often picture leaning into the love of Jesus because I have a daughter, Kaylin, who waits for me in Jesus's arms. She would have been fifteen this year. When I experienced her miscarriage years ago, I couldn't imagine a time when the events that surrounded her story wouldn't be unbearably painful to tell. I couldn't imagine thinking of her without grief stealing my breath and causing me to choke back my words. But as the Lord began to whisper to my heart about the message of this book you hold in your hands, I thought of Kaylin.

I thought about the little girl I never had the chance to hold myself, scooped up in the arms of Love, beaming with heaven's light, wrapped in an embrace of peace. I pictured her

THE LORD IS CLOSE, AND

WHILE THE SITUATIONS YOU'RE

FACING MAY FEEL FAR FROM

SAFE, YOU ARE SAFELY HELD

BY ARMS THAT WERE ONCE

SPREAD OUT ON A CROSS

SO THEY COULD WRAP YOU

UP FOR ALL ETERNITY.

hugging Jesus's neck, fully trusting Him, without any fear or pain or sadness.

I could almost imagine Kaylin smiling, saying, *It's time to tell our story, Momma.* I have told a lot of stories, but the testimony Kaylin and I share is this: She and I are both held by Jesus in this very moment. The same God who holds her in eternity, holds me right here today. Her testimony, even though she never took a breath outside my body, is the testimony all God's children have in Him: "He tends his flock like a shepherd: He gathers the lambs in his arms and carries them close to his heart" (Isaiah 40:11). That's your testimony too, Momma. You are held by Jesus.

I know life has been a lot and you feel a little bit of everything these days. I know you carry so much. I know it has been heavy. I know you're tired. I know you haven't had a chance to stop and fully heal. I won't pretend to know your story, but I do trust that the One who does know everything has so much He wants to tell you about what it means to live carried close to His heart. I know that is where we find true rest.

So, let's learn what it means to lean into the arms of the only One who can hold it all. Let's take a deep breath and accept the Lord's invitation to come experience healing rest.

LET'S PRAY

Lord, thank You for the opportunity to walk together through this season of life. I'm grateful that You are with us, and I'm grateful for the hope that comes from simply remembering that other women really do understand what I'm going through. I pray that You would reveal truth to our hearts in the pages ahead. I pray that we will find life-changing peace in the promise of Your presence. I ask that You'd work within us to soften the hard places and bring life back to the dry, numb, or weary parts of our souls. We need rest. We know it, and so do You. Help us find all that we need in You. We ask in Jesus's name, amen.

Scriptures to Pray When Life Feels Like a Lot

- "I remain confident of this: I will see the goodness of the Lord in the land of the living. Wait for the Lord; be strong and take heart and wait for the Lord" (Psalm 27:13–14).
- "I cry aloud to the Lord; I lift up my voice to the Lord for mercy. I pour out before him my complaint; before him I tell my trouble. When my spirit grows faint within me, it is you who watch over my way" (Psalm 142:1–3).
- "The Lord gives strength to his people; the Lord blesses his people with peace" (Psalm 29:11).

Rest in This Truth

I'm not alone on this journey. The Lord promised to be with me always. The Spirit of God fills my heart and surrounds my life. Even on the hardest days, I can rest in the truth that I'm safely held by a good God who loves me.

Chapter 2

WHEN YOU KNOW THE WORLD ISN'T SAFE

The Presence of Peace in a World Far from Perfect

I WHIPPED OUR BLACK HONDA ODYSSEY INTO THE DRIVEWAY AND SLAMMED the gear into park, issuing strict instructions to my three kids as we all dashed into the house: "I'm going to clear a path to the tornado shelter in the garage and open the shelter door. Grab your bicycle helmets and pillows if you want them. Then come to the shelter. We only have a few minutes!"

Born and raised mostly in Oklahoma, my family understands the threat of severe weather. We know when to be alert, when to take action, and when (and when not) to panic. On this day in late spring, as the kids scurried into the house, released early from school for the day, we were all aware of the severity of the approaching storm.

The town sirens blared their ominous warning. The winds outside howled. The TV stations had broken from their normal afternoon broadcasting to track the tornado-warned storms through the state. This wasn't a drill. My husband called from work at the fire station to tell me a tornado had been spotted just south of our rural community, and we had less than ten minutes until it was predicted to pass over our home.

I shoved the Christmas-decor boxes out of the way and heaved open the massive steel door to the shelter built beneath my garage. The trapped, dank air wafted out of the small, dark space. No matter how nice or modernized, storm shelters aren't comfortable places to spend much time. Spiders and other creatures often find their way inside. As much as I dislike anything with eight legs, that afternoon I didn't care about the cobwebs. I flipped on the light switch, raced down the stairs, and made sure spiders were the only living things sharing our shelter.

"The TV said it's not far, Momma!" my middle schooler shouted from down the long hallway in the house.

"Has anyone seen the cats?" my daughter hollered.

"I'm scared!" my seven-year-old son whimpered from the top of the shelter stairs.

"We're going to be okay!" I called back to all of them as I

raced back up the stairs into the garage. "But I need you all to come get into the shelter now!"

The garage door shook from the changing air pressure outside as all three kids bolted toward me, carrying our two young kittens. I met them and ushered them down the steel staircase that descended into the dimly lit cinderblock cellar.

With everyone secure (three brave kids and two not-so-calm scaredy cats), I climbed back up into the fluorescent lights of the garage, listening for the TV, hoping to make out where the rotating storm was currently positioned or where it might be headed.

"I'm just going to look one last time at the TV. Stay here. I'll be right back."

I dashed down the hall into the living room, shouting back to the kids, "I'm okay! You're okay! I'll be right back!" I just needed to hear what the news station was saying.

There are two things you need to know about Oklahomans. The first is that it's hard to get us down in those shelters until we are certain the storm is in our backyard (and even then, we'd probably still like to take a video of it). And second, we trust our local meteorologists like our lives depend on them . . . because they often do!

So that afternoon, when our tiny town in Northwest Oklahoma popped up on the map of all three major news stations with clear instructions to go to the lowest and innermost parts of the house, I believed them and hurried my hiney back to my babies belowground.

"I'm coming back!" I yelled ahead to my kids so they would hear me coming before they saw me running. "This will all be over soon," I reassured them as I climbed down the stairs.

And it was.

We listened as the winds weakened. The storm stopped. The sirens silenced, and the all-clear tone called out that we could safely resurface.

It wasn't the first time we had sought shelter from a threatening storm. It wouldn't be our last time either. Storms are just part of life in Oklahoma. I suppose in some ways, storms are just part of life no matter where you live (or the weather outside).

STORM SPOTTING

If I asked you to describe the current storm you're facing, I'm sure you could. You may have even thought of it as I told the story of how we took shelter. It doesn't take much for us to make the jump from the winds outside in my story to the swirl of events you face from Sunday to Saturday. We don't have to be professional meteorologists to spot the torrents in our lives. We know when the skies in our lives look ominous.

Maybe you're facing a storm in a relationship. Perhaps you're struggling with your husband or ex-husband, with your children, with extended family members, with coworkers, or with someone in your community. Maybe your storm is emotional, or perhaps it's physical. Maybe you've been dealing with sickness. Maybe you're facing a storm in your own mind. Perhaps your storm has come up unexpectedly, or maybe you feel like you're living in a state of constant wind and stress. Oh, the longing we hold in our hearts for an extended season of calm, clear skies. Amen?

We think, *If only these storms would still, then I would have peace.* If that situation, the one (or ones) you thought of as I asked you to spot the storms in your life, would disappear, then maybe you'd be able to relax.

The truth is, while we think it would be much easier to rest if the skies would clear, there's a story found in the Gospels about Jesus napping in a boat that calls into question the need for still waters to experience rest. This particular story reminds us it's not the absence of the storm that assures our safety; it's the presence of the One who rests, even on the waves, who promises our peace.

GALES OVER GALILEE

I've heard it said that, during Jesus's lifetime, the weather surrounding the Sea of Galilee created the perfect conditions for sudden squalls. This basin of water rests well below sea level, and the warm, wet air likely mingled with the cool air from the steep hills surrounding the sea to create those infamous biblical storms. I'm no expert, but maybe something about the shallow depth of the water made for even more furious waves. It was onto this windy and wildly wavy water that Peter stepped out of the boat in Matthew 14.

Do you know that story? According to Matthew's gospel, Jesus sent His disciples ahead of Him in a boat to cross the lake, but a sudden storm came up and the winds blew against them. Jesus went out walking to them on the water, and the group first believed He was a ghost when they saw Him moving toward them. But Jesus called out, "Don't be afraid. . . . Take courage. I am here!" In response, Peter said, "Lord, if it's really you, tell me to come to you, walking on the water." And Jesus said, "Yes, come" (vv. 27–29 NLT).

Peter stepped out of the boat onto the water (though my mind has a hard time picturing what that must have looked or felt like) and started to walk toward Jesus. But when he remembered the big waves and realized what was happening, he started to sink. He called out to Jesus, and Jesus immediately caught and saved Peter. The two of them walked back and climbed into the boat together.

Listen, I firmly believe that Peter is the only person to walk on water not once but twice. First, as he walked toward Jesus, and second, as Jesus pulled him back to his feet and they walked back to the boat shoulder to shoulder. You'll never convince me that Jesus dragged Peter half in, half out of the water and then heaved him back on board.

Matthew 14:32 says, "When they climbed back into the boat, the wind stopped" (NLT). And the disciples worshiped

Jesus. I love this story. There's so much we can learn from it. I've pointed to this passage of Scripture in other books I have written. However, I have never stopped to consider how Peter came to possess the faith to believe that if Jesus walked on water, then he could walk on water too. But I think the answer is in another story found in Matthew 8—the first night the disciples learned Jesus had power over wind and waves.

We read in Matthew 8 that after a long day of healing the sick, casting out demons, and teaching about the kingdom of God, Jesus and His disciples pushed out in boats to cross the lake. Jesus was tired, so He rested His head on a cushion in the stern of the small boat, and He fell asleep.

Suddenly, a fierce storm came up, and the waves were so big they swamped the boat—the same boat where Jesus slept. Terrified, the disciples shouted, "Lord, save us! We're going to drown!" Jesus woke up, stood up, and "rebuked the wind and waves, and suddenly there was a great calm" (vv. 25–26 NLT).

That was the moment the disciples first learned that calming winds with a word was possible. They had seen Jesus do many miraculous things, but *this* was brand-new. Matthew 8:27 says, "The disciples were amazed. 'Who is this man?' they asked. 'Even the winds and waves obey him!'" (NLT).

I believe that Peter possessed the faith to step out of the boat in Matthew 14 because he had already witnessed that storms are no match for Jesus in Matthew 8. I wonder, What

**JESUS DOESN'T PROVE
HIS LOVE FOR US BY
REMOVING THE STORMS.
HE PROVES HIS LOVE
AGAIN AND AGAIN BY
MEETING US IN THEM.**

storms have you already watched Jesus calm? What stories have you already lived? What have you seen God do that you could remember right here today? Peter knew that Jesus had power over the physical world around him. The lesson he had yet to learn was that Jesus doesn't prove His love for us by removing the storms. He proves His love again and again by meeting us in them.

In Matthew 8, the night Jesus slept in the boat, Jesus knew about the wind and the waves before those aboard began to cross to the other side of the lake. He knew water would fill the boat. He knew the fear His friends would face. He knew the exact moment they'd cry out for His help. So He made sure He was in the boat with them when they needed Him most. He made sure they didn't cross that lake alone. He got into the boat first. He invited the disciples in. And then He got them safely to the other side.

And Jesus knew about the second storm in Matthew 14 too. This time, He made the disciples get into the boat and go to the other side ahead of Him. He knew the wind would be against them, and He'd come walking to meet them not far from the shore. He knew Peter would step over the side of the boat and would begin to sink. And He knew He would be close enough to catch Peter and help him get back aboard. He knew it all.

I wonder: Have you ever felt as if Jesus didn't know what

was happening in your boat? Like He was either asleep or absent because He clearly didn't care?

Have you ever thought, *If He loved me, He'd pay better attention to this storm and do something about it. If He loved me, He'd stop these swirling winds (and worried thoughts) and clear the air that is thick with torrential rains. If He loved me, He'd [_____].*

What did you think of just then? What would He do for *you*?

My friend, so easily we forget. Jesus is the King who came close so we never have to face a single storm alone.

Jesus's love was proven once and for all when He willingly left His throne in heaven and was born so He might die as the perfect sacrifice—forever removing the separation that came between a perfectly holy God and an absolutely imperfect people. He came so He could be close enough to catch us whenever we might call out.

And just like He knew each storm His friends would face before they got into the boat, Jesus knew every single storm of your life leading to this day, in this month, in this year, when you would need Him in this way. He knew all the ways the water would fill your boat. He knew all about the fear you'd face and the deep need for peace you'd experience. And He knew the exact moment you'd call out for Him: "Jesus! Help!" So He made sure He was with you in this storm, knowing exactly what it would cost *Him* to be close enough to catch you.

JESUS KNEW EVERY

SINGLE STORM OF YOUR

LIFE LEADING TO THIS

DAY, IN THIS MONTH, IN

THIS YEAR, WHEN YOU

WOULD NEED HIM IN

THIS WAY; SO HE MADE

SURE HE WAS WITH

YOU IN THIS STORM.

THE COST TO BE ON BOARD

Genesis 1 talks about the creation of the world. At the command of God's voice, the sky, planets, moons, grass, fruit, oceans, and creatures came into existence simply because He said so. With just a word, He spoke and everything He made *was*. But these weren't the only words spoken during creation. A very important conversation is recorded in Genesis 1:26–27:

> Then God said, "Let us make human beings in our image, to be like us. They will reign over the fish in the sea, the birds in the sky, the livestock, all the wild animals on the earth, and the small animals that scurry along the ground."
>
> So God created human beings in his own image.
> In the image of God he created them;
> male and female he created them. (NLT)

This conversation held in heaven as God decided to make human beings included an unspoken divine decision. God, in His infinite knowledge, knew the children created in His image would fall into temptation. He knew they would disobey the one command He gave them: "You may freely eat the fruit of every tree in the garden—except the tree of the knowledge of good and evil. If you eat its fruit, you are sure to die" (Genesis 2:16–17 NLT).

God knew if He created people, they would eat fruit from

a forbidden tree and, in doing so, would change everything. They could no longer be close to a perfect God as they had been before they disobeyed Him. They'd be eternally separated from the God who made them just to love them. And He knew that the only way to redeem them would be through the gory death of His Son on a brutal cross. (And yet He still made the world!)

God did not make humanity and then wonder about any one of our days. He did not make the first people, Adam and Eve, and then find it surprising when they disobeyed Him. God's decision to make human beings in His image included His divine decision to redeem them—to redeem you—before the first man and woman had breath in their lungs. (And yet He still made the world!)

Momma, I hope you're following me. God knew the cost of creation. He knew that every generation after that first husband and wife would live with the consequences of a broken world. So, before He declared, "Let there be light," and light was (Genesis 1:3), He declared within His heart that *you* were worth everything it would cost for Him to come for you. Before pain entered our story, God made a promise to go to the cross that would make His presence possible in every one of our days. He went to the cross because He had already counted the cost and determined it was worth it—that you were

> BEFORE PAIN ENTERED OUR STORY, GOD MADE A PROMISE TO GO TO THE CROSS THAT WOULD MAKE HIS PRESENCE POSSIBLE IN EVERY ONE OF OUR DAYS.

worth the price He'd pay. This is the story before the story. This is the promise of peace in a world far from perfect.

Look around, my friend. Really consider it all. Consider your most recent storms. Consider your past shipwrecks.

She's going to need Me! I imagine Jesus speaking to the Father before creation.

She's going to need Me! I imagine Jesus remembering as He prepared to leave His throne and be born as a baby.

She's going to need Me! I imagine Jesus thinking as He hung on the cross, beaten, bloodied, and bruised.

She's going to need My peace when she's young and feels afraid. She's going to need My strength when she gets that news. She's going to need My hope when her world falls apart. She's going to need My joy when she slips into a sadness shet can't shake. She's going to need My comfort to move through that tragedy. She's going to need My joy to be her strength. She's going to need My love. She's going to need My presence every single day. So I'll go! I imagine Jesus declaring across the heavens.

Jesus knew what it would cost Him to be in the boat with you. (And He still came!)

Momma, God didn't promise us lives free from pain. As a matter of fact, Jesus said we would have trouble. Just before going to the cross, Jesus said, "I have told you these things, so that in me you may have peace. In this world you will have trouble. But take heart! I have overcome the world" (John 16:33). No, Jesus certainly didn't promise us lives free from trouble. He didn't promise us lives free from storms or free from boats so full of water they seem as if they might sink from being swamped. He did promise we would not experience the pain of trouble without the comfort of His presence. He did promise that if we were in trouble, He would be in the midst of our trouble with us.

My friend, do you understand why this really matters? Do you see why it's important to know the cost that Jesus was willing to pay so He might be with us? We cannot rest in arms we do not fully trust, yet Jesus's sacrificial love proves that we can trust Him for all eternity. So here's a hard question: Do you trust the Lord?

IN TROUBLE WITH JESUS

It was a few years ago. I was sitting at my desk at home in Oklahoma, leading another group of mommas through an online study of my book *Peace: Hope and Healing for the Anxious Momma's Heart*. We were halfway through a six-week study, and that night I was teaching from Psalm 91, focusing on the Lord's promised protection for those He loves.

Having led previous groups through the same study, I knew this was the week that seemed to bring tremendous healing for many mommas who took the course. Why? Because as mommas, we often run ourselves ragged trying our best to keep our kids safe. Some of us feel we can never stop and never rest and must always keep an eye out for all the danger our kids might ever face. As if then they'd be safe. As if we could prevent every bad thing from happening even though Jesus said in Matthew 6:27 that we cannot add an hour to our lives (or the lives of our children) by worrying about them. The good news is that Psalm 91 reminds us that we aren't the only ones keeping watch over our children.

In Psalm 91:14–16, we read:

The LORD says, "I will rescue those who love me.
I will protect those who trust in my name.
When they call on me, I will answer;
I will be with them in trouble.
I will rescue and honor them.
I will reward them with a long life
and give them my salvation." (NLT)

It's a relief to remember that the Lord says He is the protector of those who trust in His name. It brings my heart so much peace to remember that God rescues those He loves, because I become easily exhausted worrying about everything, and I bet you do too.

From the time our babies are little, we worry, and it doesn't seem to stop as they grow. *Is this car seat going to keep them safe? Is it safe for my baby to play with this toy, sleep in this position, eat this food? Is it safe for us to go to this park, or should we go to a different one? Is it safe for my daughter to have access to that feature on her phone? Is it safe for my son to drive home from college this weekend? Are my grown children safe?* Safe. Safe. Safe.

No group of women on earth is more keenly aware of the dangers of this world than mommas. We don't need to turn on the news. We don't need stories from across the country or globe. We know from the events that have unfolded in our own lives that there are real dangers that often keep us up at night. Yet we have the eternal promises found in Psalm 91 from a God who said He would rescue those who love Him.

I suppose that's why one momma's comment during that live teaching session grabbed my attention that night. As I was talking about the Lord's protection and our ability as mommas to find rest in Him as protector, her question in the comments section popped up on my screen.

But our kids aren't always safe. Are they?

In the middle of many messages from other women saying, "Wow!" "I needed this!" "I'm so glad the Lord goes with my kids even when I can't!" and "I'm so grateful God loves my children even more than I do!" I saw her words and heard the pain in her heart: "But our kids aren't always safe. Are they?"

I knew the answer. So did she. So do you and every other momma in that group and every momma who has ever clung to the promise of the Lord to protect those she loves.

Sigh.

No.

The very hard truth is that the world is not safe . . . at least, it's not *safe* in the way we might define the word. Brokenness entered all our stories back in the garden we were made for yet never got to live in. Jesus made a way for us to be together, but suffering and sadness and tragedy will continue until His final return. And because of that . . .

Sometimes the worst happens. Sometimes the unthinkable reaches right past our front doors. Sometimes we pray and trust, and the outcome isn't what we wanted. Sometimes hard and horrible things happen even while we are clinging to the Word of God and believing Him for a miracle. Sometimes it seems as if no one is safe, and because no one is safe, we can never rest. We wonder: *How do I actually put my trust in the Lord to protect my family and me in a world where pain is still part of our story?*

How can I really trust Him?

That's the question that sweet momma in the online study was asking that night. That's the question perhaps you're wondering even now.

My friend, I believe you already know the answer too. So let me simply remind you. It's tucked right there in the middle of Psalm 91:

> When they call on me, I will answer;
> I will be with them in trouble. (v. 15 NLT)

Momma, maybe like Peter, you have learned the lesson of Matthew 8. You know you serve a God who calms storms. You've seen Him do it in the past, so you confidently follow

Him right onto the waves. But perhaps that second lesson Peter learned, the one found in Matthew 14, is the one we both need to hold on to in this far-from-perfect world. Peace doesn't just come when the winds cease and there are blue skies. Peace is found in the presence of Jesus, who paid the highest price to hold us through every storm.

> **PEACE DOESN'T JUST COME WHEN THE WINDS CEASE AND THERE ARE BLUE SKIES. PEACE IS FOUND IN THE PRESENCE OF JESUS, WHO PAID THE HIGHEST PRICE TO HOLD US THROUGH EVERY STORM.**

I want you to think about your own children for a moment. Think about how you'd do absolutely anything to be with them if they were facing trouble. From the moment you first held them in your arms, you'd move heaven and earth if it meant keeping them from feeling alone in their fear or pain or uncertainty.

Just like I called out to my kids before I reached that tornado shelter, "I'm coming!" how many times do we call out as mommas, "I'm here! I'm here!" before we reach our children's bedrooms in the middle of the night? How many times do we pull our kids close (at any age) to reassure them, "It's okay. We'll figure this out together"?

Momma, how much more must our heavenly Father call out to us in His perfect love? *I'm here! I'm here! You're not alone.* It cost Him everything to make sure He was in the boat with you. So how can we question His love? How can we question His goodness? How can we wonder if He cares about what we're facing when He willingly laid down His life to make sure we are safely held for eternity, beginning the moment He took us in His arms?

My friend, He didn't leave you. Even when you were going through it, He didn't leave you. Even when your child or your spouse or your friend or your family member was in the midst of that storm, He didn't leave them. And if your heart is wondering *why* and your faith feels shaky and you've doubted His goodness and love because of those very hard, very painful parts of your story, then I'm asking you to reconsider what it means to be safe and how you might truly be able to rest if you knew that, no matter what comes, He is in the boat with you. No matter how your story unfolds, every day of your life and for the rest of eternity, you are forever safely held.

LET'S PRAY

Lord, sometimes we don't fully understand. Sometimes it all just doesn't make sense. We need rest, but often we feel like we can't relax—almost as if we don't completely believe You will hold us.

Lord, help us as we learn to trust You. Please help us understand who You are and what it means for You to be our protector. You promised You would be with us in trouble, so we believe You are with us in everything we are facing in this moment and in every one to come. We ask that You'd reveal to our hearts what it truly means for us to be safely held so we can rest in you. You are good. We love You. We will choose to trust You. We ask in Jesus's name, amen.

Scriptures to Pray When You Know the World Isn't Safe

- "Even though I walk through the darkest valley, I will fear no evil, for you are with me; your rod and your staff, they comfort me" (Psalm 23:4).
- "The LORD is my light and my salvation—whom shall I fear? The LORD is the stronghold of my life—of whom shall I be afraid?" (Psalm 27:1).
- "For in the day of trouble he will keep me safe in his dwelling; he will hide me in the shelter of his sacred tent and set me high upon a rock" (Psalm 27:5).
- "Keep me safe, my God, for in you I take refuge" (Psalm 16:1).

Rest in This Truth

Jesus knew I would need Him, so He agreed to come. He made a way so I'd never have to live through one storm alone or afraid. In a world that is far from safe, He promises He will always be with me, so I'll rest in the truth that I am safely held.

Chapter 3

WHEN YOU JUST WANT TO HIDE

Hope for the Moments in the Dark

"ARE YOU HIDING?" MY HUSBAND ASKED AS HE WALKED PAST OUR CLOSET door, knowing I was in there and that the lights were off.

"No!" I fired back, doctoring my voice so it didn't sound like I had been sobbing for the last thirty minutes. "Everyone knows I'm in here, and you're not hiding if people know where you are," I called back from among the clothes.

I guess I wasn't exactly telling the truth. You can absolutely hide even when people know where you are, and truthfully, I *was* hiding, just not from my family. I was hiding from my entire life, and I think my husband knew that. Jared wasn't surprised to find me in the closet. He has found me there many times before. It's my quiet retreat, my not-so-secret place to be alone. It's actually the first place my family looks for me when they need me and notice I'm not around.

When my kids were little and I had to make important phone calls as I worked from home, I'd go to my closet between the shirts and coats against the wall, letting the fabric absorb the sound of my kids in the other room. As the kids grew, the closet in all its stillness remained a sort of sanctuary for my anxious heart and overstimulated brain. Phone calls, moments of prayer, scrolling on social media—my closet has held it all and been my little refuge for well over a decade. So while it wasn't unusual for Jared to see me in the closet, it wasn't typical for him to find me inside with the door mostly closed and the lights turned off.

He didn't ask any more questions. He actually didn't say another word. My wise husband knew this was not a moment when I needed him to come in, flip the switch, and tell me it was all going to be okay *someday*. I didn't need him to join me there either. Had I needed connection, I would have sought him out. At that moment, I needed space. And Jared knew it.

The sound of his footsteps faded as he walked through our bedroom and closed the door behind him.

Quiet again.

Curled up, knees to chest, letting my tears do their cleansing work, I cried out the pain and pressure of what I had been carrying. Tears testifying to my exhaustion, weary words from my parched throat, I whispered, "Jesus, help. God, I need You."

I felt so stuck. I felt as if nothing I was trying was working, as if I was in a maze of only dead ends. Backed into a corner in so many situations, I needed God to do something about any part of it.

I sat there praying and crying until I had no more tears. Completely poured out, I laid on my side, one arm tucked under my head, wishing I had planned ahead for this emotional eruption and had brought a pillow and blanket with me. The carpeted floor seemed unreasonably hard that evening, the concrete underneath more noticeable than ever before.

Why *wouldn't* the ground feel uncomfortable tonight? My whole life felt hard on all sides. Rocklike. Unmovable. Even this place that had often been a little sanctuary for me now seemed like a stronghold. It felt like the place a person goes when they run out of other places to be. I couldn't fight against all that was happening in my life. I couldn't flee from it. I couldn't fix it. But I couldn't face it either. So I hid.

I'm wondering if maybe you have found yourself holed up and hiding recently as well. Maybe you don't go to your closet or even have a quiet space to retreat to. Maybe you sit alone in your car. Or maybe you scroll on your phone in your bed. Or maybe you are frozen while in motion. Maybe you look like you're going through your day, but your heart has become distant and you're hiding within yourself. Your family or friends see you going through the motions, but they don't really know that your heart and mind are deep in the woods.

Have you pulled away, fortifying yourself with an outward appearance of strength while inwardly pulling your knees to your heart, covering your face, and saying, "Jesus! Where are You? What are You doing, God? It has to get easier than this!"

My friend, I'm not here to flip on your light switch, hand you a box of tissues, and say, "Wipe your face. What's for dinner? Your family needs you, so you'd better figure this out and deal with your exhaustion later." I have a feeling you say that to yourself enough. You keep pushing through, forcing yourself to keep going even when there's nothing left.

No, my friend, this isn't a "here's how I did it so you can too" tutorial. I just thought that maybe we could sit together and remember what is still true in the dark. Literally. As I write these words, I have brought my laptop into my closet, back on the hard floor, cushioned this time by a cheap pillow from Amazon. (I think I'll leave it here for when I need it next.) I came here so I can look around and see what *truth* we can stand (or lie) on. What hope can we hold on to even in places like these? How do we heal when we just want to hide?

That night in my closet, my faith grew, and I experienced healing, but probably not like you'd imagine. I simply stayed there until my breathing calmed and my heart, mind, and body were ready to get up. Then I achily stood to my feet, washed my face in the bathroom sink, wiped it dry, and rejoined my family. It took about fifteen minutes.

As far as stories go, this one doesn't seem spectacular, but make no mistake: Healing took place there. Healing came as I felt the pain and presented it to the Lord rather than ignoring it. I poured out my heart to Jesus because I trusted He was listening. And then, whether it seemed like a supernatural event or not, God gave me the miraculous gift of resting in the truth that He was with me even when I couldn't feel Him. He was still fully the good God who loves me and holds me safely in the silence and the dark. That's not something we can learn when everything's good. It's not even something we can learn when we sense His nearness. We can only learn that we will trust the Lord's goodness no matter our circumstances, even when life isn't good and He feels distant.

My friend, my hope is that you will learn how to navigate to the other side of stress or disappointment or pain or worry or heartbreak. But I believe healing doesn't come only when we get out of those dark places, or even when we can sense that He's with us in the hard places. I think we move toward healing when we realize we don't have to rush through the hidden places because God is holding us there too.

I want to be clear. This story about my moment in the closet is not some *before* picture of a woman who has since put into place a practical plan to achieve more peace. It wasn't a bottom-of-the-barrel breakdown in which I realized that I had to brush myself off and make some changes so I could live out the far better plan God had for me. No, my friend. It was just an honest Monday night in the middle of a life that sometimes can be really hard.

> WE MOVE TOWARD HEALING WHEN WE REALIZE WE DON'T HAVE TO RUSH THROUGH THE HIDDEN PLACES BECAUSE GOD IS HOLDING US THERE TOO.

I'm not embarrassed to tell you that sometimes I want to hide. Hiding isn't wrong, but there is a right way to do it. Remember, Adam and Eve hid their bodies and then hid themselves among the trees from the Lord when they sinned. Humans have been hiding for so many reasons ever since. It's a natural response to feeling threatened or overwhelmed. But when we come to know the Lord, God offers us the chance to stop hiding *from* Him and instead come hide *in* Him. He becomes our living refuge.

We can declare, like the psalmist David, "You are my hiding place; you protect me from trouble. You surround me with songs of victory" (Psalm 32:7 NLT).

But how? We may easily repeat these words of David, but how do we live them? How does God become our hiding place? I believe the first step in living these words is recognizing the moments when we need to take refuge in Jesus. We learn to pay attention to our desires to run or hide or ignore our problems. We sense that shift in our hearts to "check out" mentally, physically, spiritually, or emotionally, and then rather than pretend everything is all right, or silently distance ourselves from those around us, we present our hearts to Jesus and acknowledge that we need Him. Because how does ignoring our overwhelm help us heal anyway? How does ignoring *any* pain help us heal? The short answer: It doesn't.

When our efforts aren't only focused on trying to stay happy and settled, but rather we give ourselves permission to feel deeply disappointed or frustrated or sad or concerned without worrying that these feelings are somehow a threat to our faith, we embrace our need for Jesus to hide us in His love. We accept the gift His death and resurrection made available to us, and in the process, we find a new sort of freedom from fear. We stop being afraid of feeling the rough stuff. The stuff a lot of life is made of—the trouble Jesus said we'd face together. The more time we spend in desperate need of God, asking Him to help us process how we really feel, the more natural it becomes to run to Him as a refuge.

Here's the thing: I'm not saying we should build homes in the hidden places of our lives or hearts, camping out and believing life will always be this way. That's not healthy. I'm not saying we should withdraw from those we love or those who can help us. We need one another, and often we need the help of professionals.

I'm simply suggesting that once we understand that hiding in the presence of God is healing—whether or not we sense His closeness or perceive a shift in our circumstances—we won't be afraid should we ever find ourselves back in this place again. We won't try to ignore these moments or pretend all is well. We won't be afraid of those times when we just want to hide, because we will understand that healing comes when we trust that God will meet us even in the dark. There's deep rest in that.

A kind of fierce, fortifying strength becomes infused into your faith when you say to the Lord, "I may not be able to see You. I may not be able to feel You. I don't know what will happen next, but I still believe that You are good because You are all I have, so here I am. Hide me in Your arms. Speak truth over my heart. Bring peace to my mind and my body. I need You." We will actually find peace when we allow ourselves to release the tight grip we've had on pretending we're okay—and let ourselves feel the stress or sadness or exhaustion or worry, trusting the Lord cares and will bring hope and healing. In His arms we discover that the dark doesn't have to steal our peace, because He's there too.

David wrote:

Where can I go from your Spirit?
Where can I flee from your presence? . . .
If I say, "Surely the darkness will hide me
and the light become night around me,"
even the darkness will not be dark to you;
the night will shine like the day,
for darkness is as light to you. (Psalm 139:7, 11–12)

This is the hope we hold on to in the dark: that whatever is true of God in the daylight must also be true of Him in the night. He does not change. But we cannot believe for ourselves that God is good even when we can't see Him or feel Him until the lights go out. I know that's really cheesy, but it doesn't make it any less true.

It is in the dark—whether the dark for you is a situation you are facing, a season of uncertain circumstances, or simply

THIS IS THE HOPE WE

HOLD ON TO IN THE

DARK: THAT WHATEVER

IS TRUE OF GOD IN

THE DAYLIGHT MUST

ALSO BE TRUE OF

HIM IN THE NIGHT. HE

DOES NOT CHANGE.

an overwhelming Monday—that the truth of God's goodness apart from His visible working in our lives becomes real. It's not just something we believe is true because we have read about it in Scripture or heard about it from others. It becomes something we believe because we have experienced it for ourselves.

My friend, every moment when you cried out to the Lord, He was near whether you perceived Him or not. Every moment when you withdrew and wanted to hide, He was with you in the hiding whether you realized it or not. You were upheld by His love when you were convinced it was your own strength that kept you from falling.

THE ONE WHO HOLDS US IN THE STORM

A few years ago during prayer, the Lord showed me a vision of a lighthouse in the middle of a turbulent sea. I saw a small island, just big enough to hold the lighthouse, with water surrounding it on all sides. The seas were violent, crashing waves up against the stone walls. The winds were howling. The skies were dark. And in the middle of this storm, I saw a woman clinging to the side of the lighthouse, her arms wrapped around the slippery stones, her feet standing on a small ledge, giant waves threatening to wash her away.

As this woman held on for dear life, I also saw Jesus standing behind her, holding her to the lighthouse, promising to keep her firmly in place.

I wondered, *Does she know He's there? Does she feel His presence surrounding her? Or does she think she must save herself from falling?* As clearly as the Lord showed me the image, I heard Him answer, *I am the One who holds her in the storm.*

Deep breath.

That's how you are held. That's where He is in your story right now. You may feel so numb, withdrawn, or frozen, unable to make any moves beyond your determined focus to keep from slipping beneath the waves—but the Lord has you. He is good. And He will be close and good even when you think you're holding the whole world together on your own.

The truth is, anyone can call God good when it is easy to see the evidence of His hand. Anyone can praise the goodness of God when the lights are on and the bills are paid and the kids are doing well and our marriage is solid and the friendships are happy and the work is fulfilling and our parents are healthy and everyone we love is okay. Make no mistake: God is good when every bit of this is true.

And...

God is also good and present and kind when the outcome of our expectations is nothing close to what we hoped, thought, or prayed. God is good when the money is running out and the kids are sick and our marriage is threatened or over and our friends have left and the work is demeaning and our parents have passed and life feels like a pit. God is good

GOD IS STILL
GOOD IN THE
DARK.

when the lights are out and we are certain we are about to slip from this tiny ledge right into the waves. God is still good in the dark.

A KING IN A CAVE

When you hear the name King David, what comes to mind? Maybe you think of the psalms he wrote because I just mentioned Psalm 139. But before David was the king of Israel who wrote songs for the Lord, he was a young man who kept sheep for his father. David was the youngest son of eight brothers, and he was destined for greatness. The prophet Samuel had visited David's family, and God had chosen David as the next king of Israel. This was not made known to God's people right away, so the newly anointed King David continued to keep the sheep.

At this time, Goliath, a great warrior in the army of the Philistines, Israel's enemies, taunted God's people at the front line of battle between the two nations. He said, "Choose a man and have him come down to me. If he is able to fight and kill me, we will become your subjects; but if I overcome him and kill him, you will become our subjects and serve us" (1 Samuel 17:8–9). For forty days, the Israelites cowered as Goliath called for a duel.

One afternoon, David arrived on the battlefield in time to hear Goliath's threats. He hadn't planned to face the Philistine.

He had come on assignment from his father to take food to his brothers and bring back word from the front lines. But the Lord had another assignment for David.

When David heard Goliath's challenge, he asked, "What will be done for the man who kills this Philistine and removes this disgrace from Israel? Who is this uncircumcised Philistine that he should defy the armies of the living God?" (v. 26).

In David's mind, this battle was as good as won because he knew the Lord was with him. So this anointed king of Israel carefully chose five smooth stones from a stream. With his shepherd's staff in one hand and a sling and stones in his bag, David approached his challenger. He had previously defeated lions and bears that had come after his sheep. He was confident that the Lord, who had helped him before, would help him once again. On that day, despite being offered the tunic of King Saul, David downed the great gladiator Goliath from Gath clothed as a shepherd and covered in the armor of God.

The Israelite army advanced, and the Philistine army was defeated. "And David took the head of the Philistine, and brought it to Jerusalem; but he put his armour in his tent" (v. 54 KJV). As David victoriously paraded through the cities on his return from battle, women came out to dance and sing of his success:

Saul has slain his thousands,
> and David his tens of thousands. (1 Samuel 18:7)

David was a hero.

Those songs the women sang as they marched through town weren't just an encouragement to the anointed king David; they were also a threat to the current king, Saul. Saul listened as the highest praises were placed on this young hero rather than himself, and something shifted in his heart. Ultimately, Saul would plot against and pursue David, seeking to kill him. The young victor, who had been plucked from the fields as the future king, had defeated the Philistine tormentor, and had been paraded through the streets after his incredible success, would sleep in the seclusion of hidden caves, fearful for his life.

That part of David's life isn't likely what came to your mind first when I mentioned him. We don't tend to think of David's flight first from the murderous Saul and then later from his own son. We don't think of the moments he spent on the run, hiding in forests or rocky strongholds. We'd rather think of David as the shepherd or the hero or the king or the man after God's own heart. But the hope of David's story is found not only in these highlight moments but also in how he responded to the Lord and what he believed was still true of God even when *he* was hiding in the dark:

> My heart, O God, is steadfast,
>> my heart is steadfast;
>> I will sing and make music.
> Awake, my soul!
>> Awake, harp and lyre!

I will awaken the dawn.
I will praise you, Lord, among the nations;
    I will sing of you among the peoples.
For great is your love, reaching to the heavens;
        your faithfulness reaches to the skies.
Be exalted, O God, above the heavens;
        let your glory be over all the earth. (Psalm
        57:7–11)

If you skimmed those words, go back for just a second and read them one more time. David wrote that psalm while he was in a cave, hiding for his life: "My heart, O God, is steadfast. . . . I will sing and make music." I don't know about you, but to read the words of a man pressed on all sides, hidden away, yet still confident in God's goodness, it stirs me to hope. It reminds me that the merciful God who had been with David every moment before he found himself in the back of the cave was with him even in the damp and in the dark. The Lord was his refuge. The Lord was his protector. The Lord was his deliverer. The same God who had met David in the field and in the fight would meet him there in the darkness and night. And He is with us now.

Oh, to have a heart like David's that expresses confidence in the Lord even while cornered in the back of a cave (or a closet!). Truly, it is in the places where we need God most that the unchanging truth of who He has always been, despite our circumstances, reaches into our sorrow, hopelessness, and discouragement and meets us with a promise strong enough to sustain us. The truth doesn't necessarily pull us out, but it does rush right into the heavy and the hidden. It declares, "God is still good in the cave!"

This promise is true for *you*. When you feel like your back is against the wall, when the Enemy is after your hope or your peace or your joy or your strength, when you feel discouragement attempting to consume you, then your outward confession of who you believe God to be even in that pressed place becomes a weapon. Not a weapon against your feelings but a weapon against the hopelessness that tries to attach itself to your exhaustion in that hidden place.

I know what that's like. I know how it feels to be so deep in the woods of your own worries or overwhelm, trying to find your way out and press forward, that you become exhausted to your core. I know the hopelessness that can attach itself to that hidden place where you feel all alone and out of options. And that's why I'm here to meet you with this hope for the dark, to tell you that you're not alone, to tell you that God is good and close and that He is healing your heart when you lean into Him, even if it seems like nothing is happening. See, I have spent the better part of the last decade speaking about anxiety and leading tens of thousands of women out of the forest of fear. I have gone back, again and again, to rescue women who feel lost or alone or afraid, to show them the way forward, to remind them that the Lord meets them and they're not the only ones to walk beneath these trees.

But in the process of leading women through those particular woods, I have also found that life really is made up of forests, and as soon as we find our way through one hard place, often the next challenge comes. This is why we cannot wait until life is settled to seek rest in Him. It's also why we cannot wait until life *seems* good to praise the Lord or remind ourselves of His unchanging goodness.

We can open the book of Psalms and find songs written in the backs of caves or forests or wildernesses, by a man who loved the Lord even when he was hidden away. We can confess the words that perhaps we can't even come up with on our own, praying the psalms of David:

> I cry aloud to the LORD;
>> I lift up my voice to the LORD for mercy.
> I pour out before him my complaint;
>> before him I tell my trouble.
> When my spirit grows faint within me,
>> it is you who watch over my way. (142:1–3)

As we call out to Him, we remember what was true of God in every forest or hard place before will be true of God in every current place that causes us to feel cornered. God is with us, and we can hide in Him. Momma, the Christian faith isn't about successfully skirting around the hard places, never acknowledging our need for the Lord to be our refuge or our strength. Great faith isn't portrayed as we prop ourselves up

> **WHAT WAS TRUE OF GOD IN EVERY FOREST OR HARD PLACE BEFORE WILL BE TRUE OF GOD IN EVERY CURRENT PLACE THAT CAUSES US TO FEEL CORNERED.**

and keep pushing forward. Great faith is witnessed in the wild display of confident hope and expectation that we will believe God is good and that He is close even as we sit knees to chest in the closet.

Whether you are hiding in plain sight, withdrawn into your own heart or mind, or just want to run and avoid it all, there is nowhere you can go where God's love cannot reach you. You don't have to pretend. Simply press into the One who holds you even in the dark.

LET'S PRAY

Lord, please remind us in those moments when we'd be tempted to pull away that there is nowhere we can go that Your love can't reach us. When we want to hide from our lives, help us learn to stay hidden in You. When we want to retreat, help us return to You and fall deeper into Your arms of grace. When it's all too much, cover us with Your love. When we want to hide, help us hide in You. We ask in Jesus's name, amen.

Scriptures to Pray When You Just Want to Hide

- "I love you, LORD; you are my strength. The LORD is my rock, my fortress, and my savior; my God is my rock, in whom I find protection. He is my shield, the power that saves me, and my place of safety" (Psalm 18:1–2 NLT).
- "Have mercy on me, my God, have mercy on me, for in you I take refuge. I will take refuge in the shadow of your wings until the disaster has passed" (Psalm 57:1).
- "The one thing I ask of the LORD—the thing I seek most—is to live in the house of the LORD all the days of my life, delighting in the LORD's perfections and meditating in his Temple. For he will conceal me there when troubles come; he will hide me in his sanctuary. He will place me out of reach on a high rock" (Psalm 27:4–5 NLT).

Rest in This Truth

I'm not afraid of the moments when I need to cry out to the Lord. He will meet me even when I can't sense Him close. This season won't last forever, but while it does, I will hide in the shadow of His peaceful presence. There I will find rest.

Chapter 4

WHEN ALL THE ALARMS
ARE SOUNDING

What Your Body Is Actually Trying to Say (Hint: It's Not "I'm Okay")

I STOOD IN MY KITCHEN AT 6:00 P.M. CALMLY COOKING DINNER WHILE AN average evening unfolded around me. My oldest son asked me about his basketball jersey. My youngest son played video games in the living room. My daughter requested to be driven to a friend's house. The meat sizzled in the pan, and I exhaled intentionally slow breaths, blowing air through pursed lips.

My body didn't feel settled. My heart felt flustered. My shoulders were pulled up around my ears. My stomach flipped. There was no obvious threat or danger or stress, but I was dealing with so much more than just my family's questions and the food I was cooking.

Only thirty minutes prior, the meat that had been thawing in the refrigerator had leaked out of the packaging, oozing down the cracks and into the vegetable drawers and all the hard-to-remove shelves. I'd had to pull out all the food, clean each shelf, and put back what hadn't been ruined by the spill. That was the kind of day I was having. That morning, I had learned about a tax bill that would be twice as much as I anticipated. I was notified that an important package was lost in the mail. And my husband called saying he had just run over a piece of metal about thirty miles from home, and his tire was flat. The weather forecasters were also talking about an approaching winter storm, so we should prepare for anywhere from eight to twelve inches of snow in Northwest Oklahoma.

The immediate situation around me—kids being kids and dinner cooking in the pan—was steady(ish), but all day long my brain had been perceiving and processing all the simple stressors, and my body was responding as if it faced a major emergency. I put my hand over my chest and took a deep breath, closing my eyes and focusing on what I felt. I've experienced panic attacks for years, but only recently have I stopped to pay attention to what they are trying to tell me.

The stove exhaust fan roared. My daughter prompted, "Mom? Moooom? Are you okay?" I smiled and nodded. I wanted to shoot back an easy answer. I wanted to pretend I was fine and for everyone to believe I was good. I wanted to say, "Yeah, babe. I'm okay." But I couldn't brush off what my body was saying. I couldn't even get the words to come from my mouth. I wasn't okay.

My racing heart had my full attention. I had reached a limit on what I could handle. Despite my best efforts to portray a calm, collected momma, I yelled toward the living room, "Turn that TV down!" as I shut off the stovetop and walked to my closet (of course) to take more deep breaths in the quiet darkness.

Those around me couldn't see it. Even I had missed the signs of overwhelm, but my body had been keeping track of all I had experienced that day (and in that season of life). The mental load in that moment was more than I could bear, and I buckled under the weight of it all.

Has anything similar ever happened to you? Maybe you haven't had a moment exactly like mine, but I'd guess you're familiar with feeling stressed. I bet at some point you've felt nearly buried alive by the responsibilities and to-dos and demands and requests, all while saying, "I'm good! What about you?" to whoever asked.

But if we could be honest for just a moment: *How are you, really?*

What has happened over the last few hours that may be causing you to feel even a little flustered or frustrated? What's keeping your body tense? What's putting you on edge with your family? What's making you feel stuck, like you just can't make a decision or deal with one more thing? What pressure is causing you to feel like you can't pause or rest? What's making you want to hide?

The thing is, we usually assume situations must be serious before we accept that they are adding stress to our lives. Perhaps when I asked how you really are, you first considered all the big issues you're facing. Maybe it's a health crisis or you're facing a serious challenge with your child, your spouse, or your parent. Perhaps you have recently lost someone you love or you are experiencing financial struggles, loneliness, or the arrival of a new baby. Big life events can obviously create stress, but how easy is it for you to admit that the simple daily things can be just as overwhelming? For some reason, we aren't always as willing to say that simple stressors are . . . well, stressful. We want to believe we have it all under control. We want to act like we're okay, because what would it mean if we weren't?

So I'll ask you again to look beyond the big issues in your life and think about the little situations you're facing today:

What has happened over the last few hours that may be causing you to feel flustered or frustrated? What's keeping your body tense? What's putting you on edge with your family? What's making you feel stuck, like you just can't make a decision or deal with one more thing? What pressure is causing you to feel like you can't pause or rest? What's making you want to hide?

If you were to be 100 percent honest in your answer, I have

a feeling you could fill a book with the simple things that seem to be stealing your peace. My goodness, I could too. But listen. We can't understand our need for rest if we're busy trying to convince everyone (ourselves included) that we're okay. Overlooking how we actually feel doesn't propel us to seek the refuge and rest that the Lord offers us. We can't heal from it if we don't address it.

The truth is, there's no need to wonder why we'd prefer to conceal how we feel rather than face it. That has been the human response since nearly the beginning of time. Remember?

MISSING PEACE

In the very beginning, in that perfect garden God made for His family, there was no pain, stress, problems, or fear. (Laundry didn't exist either, by the way.) The world God had made was good, and Adam and Eve only knew that which came with the presence of a perfectly holy God.

If you open your Bible or go to a Bible app and begin reading Genesis 1–3, you'll see how everything shifted for Adam and Eve, and consequently, for us too, when Eve stepped over the boundary God had put in place to keep her safe.

Genesis 3:7 says when Adam and Eve ate the fruit, everything changed: "At that moment their eyes were opened, and they suddenly felt shame at their nakedness. So they sewed fig leaves together to cover themselves" (NLT). We remember what happens next. They hid.

Afraid of what their nakedness meant, they tried to hide among the trees. Then God called out to them, "Where are you?" (v. 9 NLT). Adam answered, "I heard you walking in the garden, so I hid. I was afraid because I was naked" (v. 10 NLT).

I love the Lord's response to the first recorded fear in history because it already shows how Love Himself covers fear and shame. God had a conversation with Adam and Eve, and then Genesis 3:21 says, "The LORD God made clothing from animal skins for Adam and his wife" (NLT). He covered them.

I suppose it would be easy for us to believe that Adam and Eve hid and attempted to cover themselves with fig leaves because they felt shame for their exposed skin. That makes sense to us today because when we think of nakedness, we think of the clothes that cover our bodies. But I believe Adam and Eve covered themselves because they realized something that had been there before had gone missing.

When God made Adam and Eve, they were clothed in the righteousness of God's presence. They were covered by His goodness. And I believe that the instant they sinned and separation came between them and God, they looked down and realized the covering of His peace, protection, love, and safety no longer surrounded them. I'm not sure there would be a reason for Adam and Eve to be embarrassed about their bodies, but I can understand why they would want to conceal their missing *peace*.

So they did their best to cover themselves; but the Lord didn't allow them to keep their own covering. Instead, *He* covered them. He killed innocent animals as a result of their sin and made clothing for them. This covering wasn't a replacement for His presence or His righteousness, but it was the first evidence that only God can cover our hearts. When Jesus died for us, He offered a permanent covering. Isaiah 61:10 says, "For he has dressed me with the clothing of salvation and draped me in a robe of righteousness" (NLT).

Why am I talking about clothing? Because I wonder: Do we ever try to conceal that we, too, look down and feel shameful about our lack of peace? Do we ever try to cover up that we are missing the confidence of His presence? Do we try to stitch together our security or rest in our own ways by our own methods, attempting to replace with our abilities what only God can provide by His Spirit?

Listen, just as we discussed in the last chapter, we don't have to conceal that we're not okay. We don't have to pretend we don't need Him or the help of the people He sends to us. He knows we need Him. It's why He willingly gave His life as an innocent sacrifice so our sin could be eternally covered by His offering and our shame could be replaced with His grace.

The Lord knows exactly what it means for sin to have brought brokenness into the world and our bodies. He is aware that the bodies He designed to know only His presence now know stress and fear. He warned Eve of what would happen when He told her not to eat the fruit. So of course He's not surprised that we feel overwhelmed at times. I want to be very clear. God is not disappointed that you need Him. He doesn't want you to try to stitch together some makeshift covering of rest when He has already given His life to provide you with an eternal covering of peace. We don't need to hide our missing peace from Him.

So I'll ask you again. This time, without letting the shame shush you into silence . . . *How are you really feeling?* What are your heart, mind, and body trying to tell you?

FALSE ALARMS AND SILENT THREATS

My family is well acquainted with alarms. My husband, Jared, is the fire chief in our small town. Presently, there are two full-time firefighters, and the rest of the department is made up of volunteers. This matters because whenever there's an emergency, volunteers must respond first to the firehouse and then to the emergency.

During daytime hours, the town's emergency sirens, typically used to warn of severe weather, bellow out a deep tone whenever help is needed. These volunteers go about their lives as usual until the call comes across the airwaves that help is needed . . . and then, they run!

It's quite the sight to see bankers, businessmen, welders, and mechanics all racing into the station's bays, throwing off whatever "hats" they were wearing just minutes before.

In seconds, they suit up in their bunker gear and jump into trucks with sirens screaming on their way toward those in need of their help.

Whether someone has fallen, a car accident needs their equipment, or a structure or pasture is on fire, these first responders *run* every time, no matter the emergency. The trucks pull out, the lights and sirens blare, and the team races to the location, even if it happens to be a false alarm. Even if one specific mom in one specific small town had a heater with some dust on it and turned it on for the first time one winter, and the house filled with smoke. So she called 911 and the firefighters came with lights and sirens, but it was just a dirty filter and everything was fine. Still, they *ran* just the same. (It's me. I'm that one specific mom.)

Here's the connection. I think we sometimes treat our bodies like we're dealing with false alarms when we get over-whelmed or feel anxious and can't pinpoint the problem. We think, *Sure, I've been through hard things before. Sure, I've got a lot on my plate. Sure, motherhood and life can feel heavy sometimes. I love my kids and the life God has given us . . . but I should be able to handle it all, right?* We wonder what's wrong with us for feeling this way. It's just life. *So why is my heart racing like there is an emergency? Why is my breathing quick or my frustration falling on my family? What's wrong with me?*

Momma, just because there is no obvious threat does not mean there is no emergency. There is a difference between a false alarm and an alarm about a silent danger. My husband knows about these kinds of alarms as well.

A few years ago, we were sleeping soundly when Jared's radio went off in the middle of a cold winter night. He jumped up, grabbed the sweatshirt lying across the top of our dresser, and slipped on his shoes. He was gone before I could even fully realize what was happening.

The next day, I heard from a friend about a family whose carbon monoxide detector had sounded as they were sleeping. They weren't sure it was a true emergency, but they decided to call the fire department anyway. It was good that they did. The carbon monoxide levels were dangerously high, and the situation could have ended very differently.

No one could smell it. No one could see it. No one even knew there was a problem, but the alarm saved their lives.

Our bodies often signal for help long before we realize we are in trouble. Just like that tone going out across the airwaves of our small town, our bodies call for help. The question is, Are we paying attention? Tell me if you've "heard" any of these alarms lately:

- Maybe you're not sleeping well, even though you're exhausted.
- Maybe you're sleeping more than usual, unable to pull yourself from the bed or your couch.
- Maybe you're snapping at your family, frustrated easily by simple things.

- Maybe you're feeling a little hopeless (or a lot hopeless), discouraged, or sad.
- Maybe you've got headaches more often than usual, your stomach has been upset, or you're noticing that your heart races even when you're sitting still.
- Maybe you're struggling with lack of motivation even though there's so much to do.
- Maybe you're forgetting simple things, struggling to find the right words, or misplacing your phone (only to realize it's in your hand).
- Maybe you're numb, going through the motions like you're on autopilot.
- Maybe you have absolutely no energy and your body feels like it weighs a ton—or maybe the opposite is true, and you feel like you physically cannot sit and stop moving.
- Maybe you're procrastinating, avoiding simple tasks, or feel like small issues are too hard to face.

Do any of those sound familiar? Do *all* of those sound familiar? Have you tried to tune them out and keep living like all is well? Momma, often our bodies recognize when we're under stress even if our hearts or minds don't want to admit it.

Not long ago, I got a haircut from a friend I see only once every few years. As I sat in her new salon, she pulled my long hair back in her hands and short hairs near my hairline fell out of her grip. With a knowing smile she asked, "What happened about eighteen months ago?"

I thought back. Nothing extraordinary came to mind. Then I remembered: "I had a total hysterectomy, I had the virus, and I had a book release."

"That explains all this new growth," she confirmed. "You must have lost a lot of hair due to stress during that time." My mind had forgotten about it and moved on to new problems, but there was evidence of what I had experienced. My body was still recovering from stress I hadn't even realized caused me to lose my hair. I had missed that alarm altogether.

The truth is, our bodies weren't created for stress. We weren't created for the anxiety that can be expressed in our lives as a result of stress. There is peace, hope, and rest available, but we must understand how our bodies work so we can better understand all the healing Jesus offers.

PERSONAL SECURITY SYSTEM

The human body has an entire system that continually surveys the world around us for danger and responds to it automatically. Like a home security system that is always armed and ready to react to dangerous threats, this system never turns off. It uses all our senses to perceive and process everything we experience in order to keep us safe.

It's called the *autonomic nervous system*, and this

automated alarm-and-response system is made up of two parts. The sympathetic nervous system watches for danger and triggers the body's internal response if it perceives any threat. The parasympathetic nervous system returns the body to internal stability after the threat or stressor has gone.

Around the clock, 24/7, your brain uses all your senses to ask and answer over and over, *Am I safe?* As automated as your heartbeat, your brain decides how your body will respond to all it perceives. And if the environment presents threats or dangers that are greater than your body's perceived capacity to cope, the stress response is triggered.[1] Your heart may race. Your breathing may quicken. Your palms may sweat. You may have an intense urge to leave the situation or a consuming compulsion to confront the conflict. You may even find yourself feeling tuned out or unable to make decisions. According to some researchers:

> Any physical or psychological stimuli that disrupt homeostasis result in a stress response. . . . A stressful situation, whether environmental or psychological, can activate a cascade of stress hormones that produce physiological changes.[2]

To put that plainly, we all have a window of what we can tolerate. When life bumps us outside of this zone, our bodies respond no matter how much we wish they didn't. You may be fooling everyone else into thinking you're okay, but your sympathetic nervous system notices everything. All those little things that you say are "no big deal"? They're piling up, and the system designed to keep an eye out for danger doesn't care only about big emergencies. The sympathetic nervous system may respond whether we're jumping out of an airplane or dealing with an inconvenient schedule change.

Momma, whether you're stressed or have been dealing with chronic stress so long that you're now also dealing with anxiety, I have a feeling this all sounds very familiar.

I wish I had known sooner about the importance of supporting the nervous system. Up until 2019, I wouldn't have been able to tell you anything about anxiety, burnout, or survival mode, even though I was dealing with the effects of all three. I was a worried and overwhelmed mom resigned to the idea that anxiety was just a part of who I am.

I didn't understand why my mind couldn't calm and my attention was so unreliable. I didn't understand why I struggled in simple areas in which other women seemed to excel easily. I spent much of my kids' younger years as the mom with covered countertops and an even more cluttered mind (still hoping planners could bring me peace). I felt guilty that I couldn't keep up with my housework and my kids and my life. I could envision the life I wanted; I just couldn't figure out how to make it possible. Stress continued, and I shut down. I'd feel "stuck." I'd have so much to do but would scroll on my phone rather than deal with the growing laundry pile or unopened mail. *Everything* felt too hard.

I didn't realize that I had an issue with my nervous system and overall brain health that could be helped or even healed. I wish I had known then what I know now about the way our bodies work when we are under stress. I wish I had known that when we are stressed, the command center of our brain responsible for organizing, planning, and completing tasks (along with memory function) takes a back seat to the part of the brain that just wants safety and rest.[3] So it can be hard (to nearly impossible) for the overwhelmed momma to make a plan and decide what needs to be done—not because she doesn't care, but because stress changes the way her brain functions.

I wasn't lazy. I wasn't a bad mom. I wasn't intentionally disorganized or frustrated with my family. I was exhausted, overwhelmed, and desperately in need of soul-satisfying rest and the tools to help me regulate my nervous system.

If you're identifying with what I'm sharing, let me encourage you. I know you don't want to feel the way you do. Perhaps you even blame yourself for just not being better. But it's not your fault, and you aren't alone.

I can't tell you how many women I have spoken to during the last five years who have told me they weren't always this stressed or anxious. They weren't always this worried. They weren't always hanging on by such a thin thread. But when the world changed in 2020, their bodies came under intense, chronic stress, and their nervous systems responded. And for many, they just haven't calmed.

ALARMING STATISTICS

I recently read the results of a poll conducted at the end of 2020. Almost half of the adults surveyed said their behavior had been negatively affected by "the physical and emotional toll of increased stress": "Most commonly, they report increased tension in their bodies (21%), 'snapping' or getting angry very quickly (20%), unexpected mood swings (20%), or screaming or yelling at a loved one (17%)." At that time, over 60 percent of those surveyed said they needed more emotional support than what they had received over the course of the year.[4]

If you're like me after reading those numbers, you're probably thinking, *Of course people were dealing with stress back then. It was 2020!* But what are the statistics saying now? A more recent poll of over two thousand American millennial moms found that nine out of ten "are so busy they'd jump at the opportunity to clone themselves (88%) because they're feeling burnt out and exhausted (76%)."[5]

Alarms are sounding across the country. So many of us need healing rest. We need rest for our souls, rest for our bodies, rest for our minds, and rest for our hearts. We need Jesus to lead us to professionals, and into healthy practices, and to do what only He can.

My friend, the evidence is plain. Your body may be telling you that the fear and stress are too much. The alarms may be sounding that the load is too much to bear. You may be well aware of the effects of fear on your mental and physical health.

But let me pivot your attention to the undeniable love of Jesus for *you* that compelled Him to the cross—not just His love for the whole world and you as part of the deal. But His love for *you*, His friend.

Jesus suffered so you could have a chance to experience a redeemed mind and body. Jesus didn't just pay for you to have peace and rest *someday* when this life is over, when your body wears out and you reach heaven. He paid for your peace today in the here and now. He laid down His life so you don't have to live in constant fear or overwhelm, even on days like this one.

First John 4:18 reminds us, "Perfect love drives out fear." Science agrees. Two professors at Harvard Medical School report that love "deactivates the neural pathway responsible for negative emotions, such as fear."[6] And according to *Psychology Today*, "Love is the best and most reliable challenger of fear. In whatever way it can be expressed, it can penetrate even the deepest anxieties."[7]

Momma, as the Lord leads you toward healing, He may be prompting you in His loving-kindness to seek professional counseling, pastoral care, doctoral advice, or mental health support. He may be telling you to reach out to someone you trust or to make that appointment you have been putting off. Jesus is our healer, and whether He heals you this moment or leads you to those who can help you on your journey toward health, He will be walking with you the whole way.

Can you feel His arms around you right now? Can you sense Him holding you close?

JESUS DIDN'T JUST PAY FOR

YOU TO HAVE PEACE AND REST

SOMEDAY WHEN THIS LIFE IS

OVER . . . HE PAID FOR YOUR

PEACE TODAY IN THE HERE AND

NOW. HE LAID DOWN HIS LIFE

SO YOU DON'T HAVE TO LIVE IN

CONSTANT FEAR OR OVERWHELM,

EVEN ON DAYS LIKE THIS ONE.

May each alarm that sounds in your life propel you deeper into the healing arms of Jesus. May you trust Him as He leads you to your next steps that will bring healing rest.

─────────────── **LET'S PRAY** ───────────────

Lord, we aren't okay. We don't want to keep trying to pretend that we are. We don't want to conceal that our peace is lacking. We are willing and ready to admit that we need Your help and the help of those You might send to us. Where sin brought stress and fear, I thank You for the promise of Your presence that brings peace and security. Thank You for not being disappointed in us. Thank You for wanting us to come boldly to receive Your help rather than hide and try to stitch together our own peace.

Thank You for helping us learn what the alarms in our hearts, minds, and bodies might mean. Thank You for leading us to the right doctors and professionals who can help us. So many women I know need You just as much as I do. I pause to ask You to touch them and bring hope, healing, and rest to their overwhelmed, burned-out, and anxious hearts too. We ask in Jesus's name, amen.

Scriptures to Pray When the Alarms Are Sounding

- "In my alarm I said, 'I am cut off from your sight!' Yet

you heard my cry for mercy when I called to you for help" (Psalm 31:22).

- "Return to your rest, my soul, for the LORD has been good to you. For you, LORD, have delivered me from death, my eyes from tears, my feet from stumbling, that I may walk before the LORD in the land of the living" (Psalm 116:7–9).

- "My soul faints with longing for your salvation, but I have put my hope in your word" (Psalm 119:81).

Rest in This Truth

Alarms in my heart, mind, and body may be sounding, but perfect Love casts out fear, and the Lord has hope and healing available for me even as He leads me toward those who can help. I have the gift of being covered by His peace. I am loved by a God who heals.

Chapter 5

WHEN YOUR SOUL NEEDS REST

*Leaning into the Heart-Healing
Rest Jesus Offers (And Why It's
Better Than a Vacation)*

WE PULLED UP TO THE WHITE FARMHOUSE JUST OUTSIDE CHEROKEE,
Oklahoma, and my husband and our three kids got out of the
car. I paused for one stolen second, enjoying the still silence,
before joining my family. My husband's grandparents have
farmed that land in Alfalfa County for decades, and the little
house has held many family gatherings over the years. Easter,
the Fourth of July, Thanksgiving, Christmas, and birthdays
are some of the occasions when we gather on that old rock
road. I didn't grow up in a big family, but I do have the gift of
marrying into one. And on that surprisingly warm December

day, just a few weeks before Christmas, I knew exactly what to expect when I walked through the front door.

There would be cousins and aunts and uncles and extended relatives and lots of food and loud laughter and quiet chats about life outside the farmhouse's walls. There'd be kids who skipped nap time and ate too much sugar and a ton of dishes to wash. When evening came and it was time to leave, we would all wish (perhaps even plan) to see each other more often. We'd give hugs or high fives and say our goodbyes and begin the long drive down two-lane roads back home. Our hearts would be grateful for the time spent with family and equally eager to enjoy the quiet calm of the car.

As I sat staring at the house with all that awaited inside, the first gathering of what would be a very busy holiday season, I felt I was preparing myself for more than what would come that day. I was preparing for all that would unfold in the following months.

There would be Christmas presents to purchase, performances to attend, two more gatherings planned with different parts of our family, and December birthday parties to host. Please don't misunderstand me; I'm not complaining about any of these special moments. Each one is a gift, and I have a beautiful life. However, I suppose that even the best things can be hard things too. Would you agree?

As I opened my car door, stepped out, and went around the side of the van to retrieve the casserole dish full of gluten-free stuffing from the back seat (some words I never thought

I'd put into a book!), I took a deep breath. Putting one foot in front of the other toward the family I love so much, I whispered, "We just have to get through the next few weeks, and things should finally calm down."

Get through the next few weeks . . . Truly, that's not the way I wanted to experience the holiday. Nor was it the feeling I wanted to have as my family celebrated the birth of our Savior. I wanted to strip away all the extra details that kept Christmas from feeling simple and sacred. I wanted to focus on Jesus and what His arrival meant for all of us.

He revealed that He is Emmanuel, God with us. He came so the anxious heart could experience peace. He came so the weary world could find hope and rest. He came to bring life, and life abundantly. And that year I would be so happy to experience all His birth meant for us—if I could just get past Christmas. (Are you nodding your head too? Or perhaps you're shaking it.)

The truth is, I needed Him to meet me in the middle of the season. I needed the rest that Emmanuel offers. That's something I'm confident you and I both need.

I'M FINE; IT'S FINE

Maybe you've never experienced Christmas the way I described. Maybe you look forward to the hustle of the holiday season all year long. You thrive in the middle of the festivities. You love being around all the people. If that's true, and you can't relate to my overwhelmed momma heart, you still might understand what it feels like to want to "just get past" a season or situation you're facing.

Perhaps it is a surgery or a celebration, a start date or an end date, a meeting or a farewell. Perhaps it's winter, and you're hoping spring comes quickly. Maybe it's a tough season of motherhood or life in general, and you're really looking forward to the day this trying part ends. Maybe it's a series of deadlines or to-dos. Maybe this week has been too much, this month has been too much, or the last few *forevers* have been too much. Maybe you keep saying, "I'm fine. It's fine. Things should calm down after [_____]."

The problem is, life doesn't ever really calm down, does it? Before we get past whatever is right in front of us, the next problem pops up, the next season carries its own challenges, and you realize there is no finish line in sight. This can not only be exhausting; it can also feel like hope deferred, and Proverbs 13:12 reminds us that this can make a heart sick.

I recently found an old blog post I wrote when my babies were tiny. I said, "I imagine it would be quite easy to wish away an entire childhood, wishing for six months from now. To wish from one difficult stage to the next until they are all gone. To wish for a moment when it just gets easier."

That little blogger momma was wise . . . and she was right. We can overlook all the good when we're just trying to get to the next stop on our journey, especially if the current stretch is a struggle or perhaps feels mostly like survival. I don't think it's wrong to wish for easier days, but we have to stop believing that peace will only be achieved when our lives become settled. We have to stop thinking that rest can only be found as we pause in our day or when the work's all done. We must stop placing our hope in tomorrow when the God of hope has come to fill us with all joy and peace right here, today.

WE MUST STOP PLACING OUR HOPE IN TOMORROW WHEN THE GOD OF HOPE HAS COME TO FILL US WITH ALL JOY AND PEACE RIGHT HERE, TODAY.

So how do we rest before the work is done and when the load feels so heavy? How do we rest when our hearts and minds are full of worry or doubt or grief? How do we rest when the world is unsettled or when we can't see the outcome of the trouble right in front of us? How do we rest when it seems that if we stop, the wave of all there is to do will overtake us?

We shift our focus and remember that true rest is not attached to a practice or procedure or even a position. As St. Augustine once confessed to God, "You have made us for yourself, and our heart is restless until it rests in you."[1] Momma, rest is found in the presence of a Person, Jesus Christ.

CRAVING REST

When my babies were little, I wanted to sleep more than anything. I'd wake up in the morning after being out of bed most of the night, feeling like I hadn't ever really slept. *Tired* didn't begin to describe my level of exhaustion.

Back then, I would see moms who had kids the same ages as mine and try to imagine why they didn't appear as run-down as I was. I would talk to them at the grocery store or at playdates, and they'd tell me about their plans to take their kids someplace fun or how they were beginning a DIY home project during their kids' nap times. Meanwhile, I'd be daydreaming about the nap I'd hopefully get to take once my kids finally rested in the afternoon. I'd compare myself to them and imagine just how productive I could be if I weren't so exhausted all the time. In those days, what came to mind when I thought about rest was a good night's sleep and an afternoon all to myself. I didn't know that even back then I was beginning to deal with burnout.

As my kids grew, I got more sleep, but their activities often kept me from pausing. I was chasing after preschoolers and then grade schoolers and then middle schoolers, while also working from home (and dealing with life during a global pandemic and rising international tensions).

In those days, what came to mind when I thought of rest was a break from the constant stress. So much was changing in my home and across the world, and I longed for a break from the new normal of homeschooling and doing everything I could to keep my family safe. I just wanted a moment to sit down and do nothing without feeling like I *should* be doing something else. Truthfully, those feelings have crept into almost every season of my life.

Sometimes, choosing to pause only seems to remind me of how much I still need to do. I begin to think:

I should start dinner. I should reply to that email. I should call that person back. I should check on that issue with the insurance company. I should start that next load of laundry. I should care more. I should enjoy this season more. I should be giving _____ my attention. I should . . .

I don't know about you, but even when my body takes a break, my mind often refuses to relax. Why? Because I have been taught by the world (as most of us have) that going and doing are more important than resting and being.

Now that my children are teenagers, I sleep more, but I'm still just as busy. My kids aren't small enough to tuck into my arms and keep safe, and so much of my time is spent preparing them to become the adults God has called them to be. Today, when I think of rest, I long for something deeper than a refreshing pause. I want assurance that will allow my heart to settle as I believe that God is with my children and guides their futures.

In every season of motherhood so far, no matter the ages of my children, my heart has craved more than just sleep (even though sleep would be nice). I want more than just a day off from all the responsibilities, but I wouldn't reject that if it were offered to me either. I'd love a vacation, but you and I both know real life waits for us the moment we step back through our front doors.

I have a feeling you and I both want something more permanent. We want rest that soaks into every ordinary second from Sunday to Saturday and heals those stressed-out places in our souls. We want rest that resets our nervous systems and calms our racing thoughts. We want rest we can carry with us and isn't dependent on what's happening around us. Good news: This is what Jesus said we'd find when we came to Him.

CROSSBEAMS

When I think of rest, I don't immediately think of wooden farm equipment attached to the backs of two animals so they can work side by side—but that's the analogy Jesus made to illustrate the rest He offers us. In Matthew 11:28–30, He said, "Come to me, all you who are weary and burdened, and I will give you rest. Take my yoke upon you and learn from me, for I am gentle and humble in heart, and you will find rest for your souls. For my yoke is easy and my burden is light."

Had Jesus said, "Come to Me, and let's go to My beach house, and you'll find rest for your souls," He might have painted a picture we preferred. I've thought of rest differently throughout the stages of my motherhood, but I can't say that I've ever thought of rest and farm equipment together.

Jesus would have been familiar with wooden yokes. He was the son of a carpenter, and I imagine Jesus may have watched His dad, Joseph, carefully carving a yoke out of a large wooden beam. I imagine Jesus looking on as His earthly father smoothed the edges and shaped the yokes so the animals who wore them could complete their work comfortably. He knew how important it was for the yokes to be tailor-made for the necks that would bear them. This is what Jesus meant when He said His yoke was easy. He didn't mean simple. He meant it was made for us to step into—crafted just for us.

We come to Jesus and take on His yoke. We walk with Him, the One who knows what needs to be done and how it needs to be done; the One who knows where He is going and why He is going there; the One who can carry the full weight of everything He has asked us to accomplish in His supernatural strength. All we must do is stay in step with Him. Jesus didn't say anything about a vacation. He offered us something better—soul rest.

Momma, soul rest isn't realized as Jesus removes our labors. Instead, we find it as we accept the opportunity to co-labor with the One who holds all things together. We will never find rest while trying to carry the weight of the world in our own human strength.

I can't tell you how to organize your days so you have time to take a break. But I can help you orient your heart and fix your attention on the Lord, who offers rest in the middle of all our unfinished work. He holds us close. He calms our hearts, minds, and bodies in His presence. This isn't just something nice that can be written about in a book. This is what Jesus came to do: to make sure we didn't have to bear our burdens alone. This is what propelled Him to the cross.

I wonder if, as a young boy watching His father work, Jesus thought of the wooden beam that would someday be placed on His own back—not a yoke but a cross meant for sinners. Jesus would bear the ultimate burden of sin and destroy the power of separation, making it possible for us to come close to Him.

Certainly, Jesus's audience on the day He spoke about a yoke didn't realize He would be placed on the cross when He told them, "Take my yoke upon you and learn from me, for I am gentle and humble in heart, and you will find rest for your souls. For my yoke is easy and my burden is light" (Matthew 11:29–30). But today, two thousand years later, you and I can see the full picture of what He meant. Jesus placed the massive weight of sin upon Himself so it wouldn't be placed on us. Jesus carried what we could not so we might have access to the rest we don't deserve as we abide with Him. The rest Jesus offers us doesn't come as a handout, as if we could place an order for rest and then grab it from a sack through a drive-through window. "More rest, please!"

Healing rest comes only as we stay connected to Jesus.

See, we want the rest that comes in His presence, but to stay in step with Jesus, we must follow His very clear instructions: "If anyone would come after me, let him deny himself and take up his cross and follow me. For whoever would save his life will lose it, but whoever loses his life for my sake will find it" (Matthew 16:24–25 esv).

For most of us, that's not the way we want this rest thing to work. I don't really want to lay down my way of doing things, my own expectations, or my own control. Do you? Does anyone really want to let go of control? Personally, I want the load to become lighter because Jesus picks up the other end of this heavy burden and carries it with me. I want to point Jesus toward the areas of my day and the situations I'm facing and the big emotions I'm holding and say, "Grab that side, Jesus; I'll take this one." Because I trust myself to get things done. I just want the supernatural strength that I understand Jesus offers. Sound familiar?

If He could just help me get my life under my control, I think, *then I could relax. If He could just help me organize my day, or catch up on this work, or give me more strength so I can finish my work, then I could find rest.* That's the route many of us would choose to reach rest. We want to maintain control but still gain rest. But Jesus offers a better way.

Jesus invites us to lay down our will and attach ourselves to His good work. He says, "Take my yoke upon you and learn from me" (Matthew 11:29). His yoke. His plan. His kingdom come, and His will be done . . . This is how we enter into the rest Jesus offers. We must take on His yoke and go in the direction He leads. But as uncomfy as it may be to release the tight grip we've held on how things are done, what Jesus offers us in exchange is so much better than what we've attempted to accomplish in our own strength. His burden is easy. His yoke is light. To receive rest, we must co-labor with Jesus.

The whole thing almost seems upside down, doesn't it? But the kingdom of heaven is often described in ways that would confuse the world. Scripture teaches us the first shall be last, and the last shall be first (Matthew 20:16). Whoever makes himself high will be brought low, but whoever brings himself low will be raised up (Matthew 23:12). And we must lay down our striving to pick up peace in His presence.

Please listen carefully, because what I am sharing here with you is not what the world says you need. If you look up "ways to rest" on the internet, you will find very practical ways to pause. Entire books and podcasts and magazine articles and YouTube video series are dedicated to teaching moms how to relax their minds and bodies.

Don't get me wrong; many of these practices are great. Later, we will talk about some practical steps to bring rest to our bodies. There are so many good ways to give your mind and body a break from the rush, pressures, and stressors of daily life. Pausing from our labors can be an act of worship as we declare with our actions, "I can rest in God's completed work even before mine is finished." Pausing is good.

But all the calming, restful, relaxing practices in the world cannot provide the soul rest that comes only from the presence of peace Himself. *Make no mistake: The rest that comes from the Lord cannot be separated from His presence.* (It's so important, I went ahead and emphasized it for you.) When we stay connected to His heart, He offers rest like an infusion of His supernatural peace directly into our souls.

We can rest in Him as we remain with Him because Jesus's rest isn't a reward for our finished work; it's a gift He offers through His finished work on the cross.

Right here. Right now. Emmanuel, "God with us," has come (Matthew 1:23). Don't rush by Him. Don't wait for a break in your schedule to respond to His prompting in your heart. God came so He could be with us and make *available* everything we might need. It's our job to *receive* it. It's our job to step beneath His yoke, yield, and learn from Him. His yoke is a gift, not a burden.

> JESUS'S REST ISN'T A REWARD FOR OUR FINISHED WORK; IT'S A GIFT HE OFFERS THROUGH HIS FINISHED WORK ON THE CROSS.

I've said it before, but I'll say it again. That tight grip you have on everything—it's exhausting, isn't it? You've done your very best to hold everything together for everyone. The Lord knows you have been stressed. He knows you have been anxious. He knows you have been overwhelmed. He doesn't want you to do it all on your own. You may have felt like you've been holding it all together, but only He can carry it all. Momma, maybe it's time to let Him.

REST GOES WITH US

Remember the baby, Moses, put into the basket by his momma? The one the Lord safely held until he was rescued

THE REST THAT COMES FROM THE

LORD CANNOT BE SEPARATED

FROM HIS PRESENCE. WHEN WE

STAY CONNECTED TO HIS HEART,

HE OFFERS REST LIKE AN INFUSION

OF HIS SUPERNATURAL PEACE

DIRECTLY INTO OUR SOULS.

from the water? That baby grew to be a man who knew the Lord as a friend and recognized that God's presence makes all the difference.

As Moses led God's people out of Egypt, where they had been enslaved for more than four hundred years, he said to the Lord, "You have been telling me, 'Lead these people,' but you have not let me know whom you will send with me" (Exodus 33:12).

The Lord answered, "My Presence will go with you, and I will give you rest" (v. 14). That sounds pretty similar to what Jesus said, doesn't it? Two thousand years later, Jesus spoke in Matthew 11:28, "Come to me . . . and I will give you rest."

Across Scripture and generations, the Lord promises that His presence brings rest. This truth remains for you and for me. God is with us and offers us peace in His presence. In this very moment—arms extended, pierced hands beckoning—He is whispering to you, specifically by name: *Come find rest.*

Let's do something together. Let's shift our focus one more time and remember just how close Jesus really is.

Imagine with me for a moment that you look up and see Jesus walking through the door nearest to you. Perfect Love fills the space. He's there just to speak to you.

You inhale deeply, and peace fills you like warm, sweet air. It spreads through your whole being.

As Jesus comes closer, everything else goes out of focus. You're captivated by His face, and you feel calmer just seeing Him. But He doesn't just stand there nearby. He opens His arms, and you fall into Him. There's so much you want to say, but He already knows. Your heart beats in rhythm with His. Your chest rises and falls in sync with His every breath. The tension in your body has released, the fear has melted, the worries quiet, and you really do feel safe.

You're not looking forward to tomorrow. You're not replaying yesterday. You're right here, right now, with Him.

Don't rush on. Close your eyes. Listen. Pause for a moment to become aware of His presence.

It's in a moment of connection with our Creator that we realize how much of our lives are spent distracted from Him, unaware of His presence. Desperately needing Him, we look everywhere else for the rest that only He offers. Busy, perhaps, with even the best things but neglecting the one thing that is needed.

What do you need to tell Him? What do you need Him to do for you? What heaviness do you need Him to take? It has been so much, hasn't it? It has been so . . . so heavy. And you have been so strong and such a good mom. *Really.* You have tried so hard and carried so much with tremendous grace under pressure.

I want you to imagine that, as the Lord holds you, you have in your hands those things you've held so tightly. You can't hold both. You cannot keep your grasp on them while also clinging to Jesus. So He gently places His hand over yours. He holds His other hand underneath, and He kindly slips those things you've been carrying into His own love-pierced hands.

As you let go, you realize how heavy those burdens have been. He knows. He loves you, and He cares so deeply about everything you've been trying to deal with on your own. Momma, your job is to receive the rest He offers. Your job is to stay in step with Him. His job is everything else.

Do you hear Him whispering to you right now?

Come to Me . . . because I know you have been carrying the mental load for your family.

Come to Me . . . because I know you're burned-out and exhausted.

Come to Me . . . because I know you have tried and tried on your own.

Come to Me . . . because I know you want wisdom, and Google doesn't have all the answers.

Come to Me . . . because your mind and your body need total restoration.

Come to Me . . . because I am your healer and your hope.

Come to Me . . . because I am the Savior of every part of your story.

"Come to me . . . weary and burdened, and I will give you rest" (Matthew 11:28).

--------------------- **LET'S PRAY** ---------------------

Lord, we respond by doing just that. We pause right here to ask You to remove the burdens of our own expectations, efforts, and ambitions. We let go and trust You. Teach us how to walk with You step-by-step, day by day. Teach us how to wake up and remember You are near. You are humble, and we want to be like You, so we humbly ask for any stubborn resistance in our hearts to be supernaturally released by Your Spirit. We don't fully understand what it looks like to remain with You and gain rest from You, but we are willing to learn. Please teach us. Thank You for what You have done for us. Thank You for Your love. We ask in Jesus's name, amen.

Scriptures to Pray When Your Soul Needs Rest

- "The LORD is my shepherd, I lack nothing. He makes me lie down in green pastures, he leads me beside quiet waters, he refreshes my soul" (Psalm 23:1–3).
- "As the deer pants for streams of water, so my soul pants for you, my God. My soul thirsts for God, for the living God" (Psalm 42:1–2).
- "Why, my soul, are you downcast? Why so disturbed within me? Put your hope in God, for I will yet praise him, my Savior and my God" (Psalm 42:11).

Rest in This Truth

Jesus's way is better than anything I could take care of on my own. I don't need to have everything under control. I just need to trust the One who holds the world, and me especially, in His capable hands. His presence changes everything. I will remain with Him so I might rest in Him.

Chapter 6

WHEN YOUR BODY NEEDS REST

*Hope for the Momma Who Is
Tired, Hungry, and Discouraged*

OVER A DECADE AGO, I WALKED INTO A CHICK-FIL-A AND WATCHED AS ANOTHER young mom stepped up to the counter with a baby and two small children. With my own three kids in tow, I saw a very familiar sight unfold. This momma had one baby on her hip and two others running around her legs. I could tell just by watching that she had so much on her mind. Studying the menu, adjusting the baby and her diaper bag, keeping an eye on the little guy inching closer to the people in front of them in line, and listening to her little girl ask what I'm sure was the hundredth question since they'd entered the building, this momma somehow gave each need her full attention.

Back then, at least at the Chick-fil-A in our area, CFA team members didn't bring the food to the table for guests. So I watched as the momma ordered lunch, received their drinks, and somehow managed to get a baby, toddler, and young child with their meals to a table near the indoor playroom. She did it all without tears or spills. I would have helped, but my own hands were entirely full. So all I could offer was admiration and an understanding smile from afar.

In just a moment, it would be my turn to balance my way to our lunch table as well. Hopefully, I would manage with just as much grace. But if I remember the day correctly, I didn't. There were dropped straws and fights over who would sit where and french fry containers that seemed unevenly filled. It was a typical lunchtime out. We hadn't gone with friends that day, but I was surrounded by good company.

Moms just like me were opening sauce packets, unwrapping straws, and carefully handing juice boxes to little hands that would undoubtedly squeeze and spill and need to be wiped. These mommas spent so much time preparing food for and cleaning up after their kids, many didn't get to eat. Just as they were about to take a bite, the kids declared they were done or the baby got fussy or someone wanted to go to the play area. I watched so many women box up their own nuggets, probably planning to eat them later.

My children are much older now, but I can't tell you how often I still take care of the needs of my children before taking care of my own. I may skip lunch to run family errands or spend my evening driving kids to after-school events rather than resting my body. I may sit up late and talk with one of my kids who needs to share their heart, knowing I won't be able to get the work done I had planned to take care of once they were asleep. I'd sleep, but it would be later.

Truly, I thought this was something that mostly impacted mothers with younger children. Of course a newborn will need to eat, so momma will have to eat later. Of course a crying toddler might need to be calmed, so momma will sleep later. As our children grow, putting our kids' needs ahead of our own might not need to happen as frequently—but I have also seen my own mom with her grandkids. I guess it doesn't ever really stop. We just keep putting others before ourselves. The thing is, even while we are focused on everyone else's needs, the Lord knows exactly what *our* needs are right now.

DINNER AND A LESSON

Jesus's disciples experienced what it feels like to put their own physical needs after the needs of others too. In Mark's gospel, we read about a time when the disciples were hungry, exhausted, and surviving an emotional roller coaster.

Jesus had sent them out to heal the sick and preach about the kingdom of God. They came back with tales of all they had done, but there was other news: Jesus's relative John the Baptist had been killed by King Herod.

John was special. He was part of Jesus's family and many of the disciples' first rabbi. They knew him. The cared about him. And when he died, they mourned for him alongside Jesus.

Yet the pressing needs of the persistent people continued. The crowds kept bringing their sick and disabled to the Lord. Scripture says, "Then, because so many people were coming and going that they did not even have a chance to eat, he said to them, 'Come with me by yourselves to a quiet place and get some rest'" (Mark 6:31).

I bet you'd love for Jesus to say the same thing to you. Wouldn't that be something? For Jesus to say, "Hey, you haven't had a chance to eat. Come with Me to a quiet place and get some rest"? Now imagine the disappointment you might feel if you went away with the Lord, expecting a retreat, and instead found five thousand people waiting for you. That's exactly what happened to Jesus's friends.

Mark 6:32–33 says, "So they went away by themselves in a boat to a solitary place. But many who saw them leaving recognized them and ran on foot from all the towns and got there ahead of them." Jesus saw the needs of these people as well. He had compassion on them too.

As the end of the day came, Mark's gospel records that Jesus's disciples came to Jesus and said, "This is a remote place . . . and it's already very late. Send the people away so that they can go to the surrounding countryside and villages and buy themselves something to eat" (vv. 35–36). Jesus had another solution. "You give them something to eat," He answered (v. 37).

I can't even imagine what emotions must have washed through the disciples in that moment. What they didn't know was that Jesus was about to feed them both physically and spiritually.

The disciples found a boy with a few fish and a few loaves of bread and brought them to the Lord. Jesus supernaturally multiplied them so there was enough for everyone to eat. When we read this miraculous story of how one boy's small offering fed over five thousand people, we often focus on how wonderful it was for Jesus to take so little and spread it so far. We apply this lesson to our own lives and say, "The Lord can take what little we place in His hands and multiply it too." I've pointed out this truth in my other books. But today, I want to shift your attention.

See, Jesus wanted His disciples to eat, but He wanted to fill them spiritually as well. We miss that part of the story. We miss the part where these guys were so tired that Jesus recognized they needed some time alone—so He invited them to come away and eat and rest. Yet they ended up lugging baskets of fish and bread to thousands of people and feeding everyone who was hungry. They were likely still exhausted in every way, emotionally, mentally, and physically, yet they still did what Jesus asked them to do. They just kept loving Jesus by loving the people He put in their path to care for. And they were blessed by it.

After all, the disciples ate the miracle meal too. Mark records, "They all ate and were satisfied" (6:42). Listen, I don't know what they usually ate. I don't know what they had intended to eat that evening. But I imagine the meal they did eat was one they'd never forget.

The disciples ate later than expected, but they definitely ate better bread—miraculous bread. Bread that reminded them that Jesus could provide for every single need they could ever have. It was dinner and a lesson.

I believe *this* was Jesus's plan all along. Jesus wasn't just inviting His disciples to a retreat because He had noticed they needed physical rest. Jesus was inviting His disciples to receive the rest that can only be found when we realize that He supernaturally cares for and meets every single one of our needs, physically and spiritually.

I love that everyone present that evening had their hearts and bodies filled when they came to Jesus. Those in the crowd came for a lesson and received a meal. Jesus's disciples went away with Him to eat and received a lesson to go with it.

Momma, the message I want you to grab hold of here is the same message Jesus shared with His closest friends that evening. There is rest for your heart as you trust that Jesus supernaturally cares for and meets every single one of your needs, physically and spiritually.

FED BY A RAVEN AND A WIDOW

The feeding of the five thousand is not the only example of the Lord supernaturally feeding those He loves and cares about. Jesus supernaturally fed four thousand people on another occasion, and God fed tens of thousands of Israelites as they traveled through the wilderness on their way to the promised land. He has miraculously fed multitudes, and He has miraculously provided food for just one. The story of God's provision in the prophet Elijah's life reminds us He already has a plan to bring us exactly what our bodies need.

Elijah served the Lord as a prophet during a time when the people of God worshiped false idols. Israel's kings committed evil in the sight of the Lord and led Israel to sin against God. First Kings 16:13 says, "They provoked the anger of the LORD, the God of Israel, with their worthless idols" (NLT).

Elijah spoke a drought over the land, promising no rain would fall until he gave the word. Then the Lord said to Elijah, "Leave here, turn eastward and hide in the Kerith Ravine, east of the Jordan. You will drink from the brook, and I have directed the ravens to supply you with food there" (17:3–4).

Elijah did as the Lord asked, and the Lord sent the ravens: "The ravens brought him bread and meat in the morning and bread and meat in the evening, and he drank from the brook" (v. 6). This continued until the brook dried up and the Lord said to Elijah, "Go and live in the village of Zarephath, near the city of Sidon. I have instructed a widow there to feed you" (vv. 8–9 NLT).

Elijah again did as he was directed. He arrived in Zarephath to find a widow gathering sticks: "He asked her, 'Would you please bring me a little water in a cup?' As she was going to get it, he called to her, 'Bring me a bite of bread, too'" (vv. 10–11 NLT). She didn't protest giving him water, but

THERE IS REST FOR

YOUR HEART AS YOU

TRUST THAT JESUS

SUPERNATURALLY

CARES FOR AND

MEETS EVERY SINGLE

ONE OF YOUR NEEDS,

PHYSICALLY AND

SPIRITUALLY.

providing the bread would be a little trickier. She had none in her house, and she had been out gathering sticks so she could cook the final meal for herself and her son. But Elijah encouraged her. He said, "Don't be afraid. Go home and do as you have said. But first make a small loaf of bread for me from what you have and bring it to me, and then make something for yourself and your son" (v. 13).

The Lord had told Elijah that this woman's jar of flour and jug of oil would not run out until rain returned to the region. With her heart full and the promise of full bellies for her and her son, this widow did what Elijah instructed. And the Lord was faithful. The flour and the oil never ran out while the drought continued.

Once again, the Lord had provided exactly what Elijah needed and provided for those with him as well. Elijah had been fed by ravens. He had been fed by a widow. Not long after, he'd be fed by an angel. The Lord provided for Elijah because when God calls us to an assignment, He has already baked in His provision so we might be able to accomplish that assignment with Him. My friend, God knows what your body needs, and He has a plan in place to provide for you.

FED BY AN ANGEL

Scripture tells us that in the third year of the drought, the Lord directed Elijah to present himself to Israel's King Ahab. This man ruled over God's people, but he had a wicked heart and served the false god Baal.

Elijah posed a challenge to the evil king: "Summon the people from all over Israel to meet me on Mount Carmel" (1 Kings 18:19). Ahab was also to bring 450 prophets of Baal. Once everyone was assembled on Mount Carmel, Elijah called out, "How long will you waver between two opinions? If the LORD is God, follow him; but if Baal is God, follow him" (v. 21). When the people said nothing, Elijah said:

> I am the only one of the LORD's prophets left, but Baal has four hundred and fifty prophets. Get two bulls for us. Let Baal's prophets choose one for themselves, and let them cut it into pieces and put it on the wood but not set fire to it. I will prepare the other bull and put it on the wood but not set fire to it. Then you call on the name of your god, and I will call on the name of the LORD. The god who answers by fire—he is God. (vv. 22–24)

Baal's prophets called out with no answer. Then Elijah had his sacrifice drenched in water and called out to the Lord. The fire of God fell down and consumed "the sacrifice, the wood, the stones and the soil, and also licked up the water in the trench" (v. 38). Amazed, the people of God cried out in repentance, and Elijah directed them to seize the false prophets and have them killed.

When King Ahab's wicked wife, Jezebel, heard what had

happened to her false prophets, she hissed out a murderous threat and sent it to Elijah: "May the gods deal with me, be it ever so severely, if by this time tomorrow I do not make your life like that of one of them" (19:2). I'd like to say this is the moment when Elijah rebuked her and the wicked queen befell the same fate as her false prophets, but that's not how this story goes.

Elijah, who had experienced the miraculous provision and power of God, was terrified of Jezebel. He turned and ran for his life into the wilderness because even great men of God have nervous systems that sometimes compel them to flee from danger. After running for days, feeling overwhelmed and afraid, Elijah sat under a bush and prayed that he might die. Exhausted in every way, Elijah fell asleep, and the Lord sent help.

"All at once an angel touched him [Elijah] and said, 'Get up and eat.' He looked around, and there by his head was some bread baked over hot coals, and a jar of water. He ate and drank and then lay down again" (vv. 5–6). You might think that meal was enough to strengthen Elijah, but he didn't just need to eat. He needed sleep too. After he slept again, "The angel of the LORD came back a second time and touched him and said, 'Get up and eat, for the journey is too much for you.' So he got up and ate and drank" (vv. 7–8). This time Elijah was so strengthened, Scripture says, "He traveled forty days and forty nights until he reached Horeb, the mountain of God" (v. 8).

When Elijah was at the absolute end of himself—hiding

under a bush in the desert while mentally, physically, spiritually, and emotionally exhausted to his core—the Lord met him. He didn't just send an encourager. He sent food and water. *Twice!* God wasn't angry with Elijah for being discouraged. He wasn't upset that Elijah needed His help. God didn't rebuke the prophet for running away or even for wanting to sleep forever. In His kindness, the Lord supernaturally provided food, water, reassurance, and an invitation to meet with Him. God provided everything Elijah needed because He didn't just care about Elijah's heart. He cared about his mind and body as well.

I'm not sure what kind of heavenly bread was cooked on the coals by his head, but I bet it was delicious. I bet that water was so refreshing. And I bet that nap felt so, *so* good. Once Elijah had fully eaten and fully rested, the Lord then invited Elijah to a private meeting with Him on the mountain.

Just as Jesus provided the disciples food and an invitation to meet with Him, the Lord fed Elijah physically and spiritually. I'm so glad we have a God who cares about and provides for all our needs.

But I wonder if, like me, you've ever thought, *I'd love a nap, a snack, and a chance to meet with Jesus. When is God going to supernaturally provide for my needs?*

Momma, like the good Father He is, God knows what His children need before they even know to ask for it. He knew Elijah was hungry. He knew Elijah was thirsty. He knew Elijah was tired. He knew Elijah was discouraged. He knew Elijah was afraid. He knew Elijah didn't want to go on. In the same way, He knows all the moments when you have been hungry, exhausted, discouraged, or even hopeless.

He knows you need rest for your soul *and* rest for your body. Like Elijah and the disciples, the Lord wants to help you find moments away from the crowd to meet with Him. God created you to enjoy resting in His presence, and He knows that in the world you live in today you don't get to stop very often. This is not what He wants for you. He knows you need time to rest your body, like pausing to read a book *(hi!)* or taking a bath or going for a slow walk or stretching and breathing.

It's so important to spend time doing what reduces the effects of stress on your body, such as being in nature or exercising or journaling or talking with a friend or doing something creative. I know I'm not telling you anything new by encouraging you to take practical steps to reset your nervous system or release the tension you've been carrying. But I also know, as a momma, that sometimes—maybe even *most* of the time—everything else feels more important. It's not so much that you don't know practical ways to allow your body to rest, but that you don't know how to make *time* for your body to rest.

My friend, I want to encourage you that because we know Jesus cares about all of our needs, He cares about helping you find those moments to rest your body too. Jesus modeled in His own life what it looks like to take a break from others, get alone time with our heavenly Father, and even take a nap when needed. He was fully God and fully man and He still needed a nap. How much more do we?

I don't know if, like Elijah, you have ever been so discouraged you felt you could sleep for days . . . or possibly so discouraged you just wanted to sleep forever. I don't know if you have ever been that sad or overwhelmed or afraid, but your feelings are not hidden from the Lord. He isn't upset with you for needing Him in even your lowest moments.

I can't rush past this. Listen. If you feel like Elijah did as he hid under that bush, please tell someone. If you're beyond anxious or exhausted or discouraged, there are numbers you can call to talk to people who can help immediately (you can call or text 988 at any time, 24/7). Please contact a professional if you're in that place. But, please, also reach out to someone you love and trust and tell them how you feel.

If you aren't exactly as low as Elijah in that moment, but you relate to his physical exhaustion, the Lord knows that too. He has given us the gift of His presence and the gift of each other. He may not have sent an angel from heaven to bring you food, but I bet you can recall times when He sent people to help you when you needed them most.

I call these people in life "trail angels." They're the ones the Lord sends to help pull us out from under those bushes or perhaps bake us some bread and tuck us in for a nap and remind us we aren't alone. He sends people to pick up our kids when we can't be there or bring us food when we can't cook. He sends people to take care of those we care for or to help us with what we have to get done. He sends friends, but sometimes He also sends strangers. He sends teachers or neighbors or folks from church. He sends helpers in the grocery store and professionals who know how to accomplish those projects that require expertise. He sends doctors and caregivers and nurses in hospitals to walk with us through hard seasons or uncertain moments.

I bet if you really thought about it, the Lord would bring to your mind some of the people who have been your trail angels. Personally, I'm so grateful for those whom the Lord has placed on my path to help me on my journey. They have prayed for me, carried my burdens as if they were their own, and been the hands and feet of Jesus to me.

You know, sometimes we pray for something in our lives to change, and instead the Lord sends a person to help us carry on until things *do* change. Sometimes we think we need a whole different life, and the Lord says, *Take a nap and eat something, and you'll feel better.* I love that Jesus understands

> SOMETIMES WE PRAY FOR SOMETHING IN OUR LIVES TO CHANGE, AND INSTEAD THE LORD SENDS A PERSON TO HELP US CARRY ON UNTIL THINGS *DO* CHANGE.

what we really need because He is God, and He came to live and walk among us as a man. He knows the needs we have because He experienced them Himself.

I love picturing Jesus eating bread with His friends and sleeping in boats. He was a wonderful example of what it means to carry the power of the Holy Spirit and still bear witness to the importance of sleep and food and company to reset our hearts, minds, and bodies.

I don't know what you have been praying for. I don't know how often you think you'll just take care of yourself later. But I believe Jesus has heard. I believe Jesus wants to bring hope to your heart and strength to your body—and that help is already on the way.

Consider these thoughts with me for a moment. What do you need Him to help you with right now? What physical needs are you facing? What heaviness or discouragement have you been carrying? Who has He sent into your life to be a trail angel on your path? In what areas can you anticipate that even if He meets your needs later, it might mean His answer will be even better?

LET'S PRAY

Lord, thank You for knowing what we need before we even ask. You say in Isaiah 65 that we are people who are blessed by You and that our children are blessed as well. You say that before we even call to You, You will answer us. You say that You will answer our prayers while we are still talking about what we might need. It's easy for us to notice what we're missing but not have the time or energy to figure out how to make whatever we lack a priority in our lives. Yet You see what we need and have already sent people to help us. Help us ask You confidently for all we need, trusting You are a good Father who wants to respond. Help us not to put that off until later. Please help us find moments to rest our bodies and meet us in those moments with Your supernatural strength. We ask in Jesus's name, amen.

Scriptures to Pray When Your Body Needs Rest

- "In peace I will lie down and sleep, for you alone, LORD, make me dwell in safety" (Psalm 4:8).
- "Therefore my heart is glad and my tongue rejoices; my body also will rest secure" (Psalm 16:9).
- "Consider the ravens: They do not sow or reap, they have no storeroom or barn; yet God feeds them. And how much more valuable you are than birds!" (Luke 12:24).
- "Those who hope in the LORD will renew their strength. They will soar on wings like eagles; they will run and not grow weary, they will walk and not be faint" (Isaiah 40:31).

Rest in This Truth

God is good to me. He wants to provide for me because He is the Provider. He wants to comfort me when I'm discouraged because He is the Comforter. I will rest in the promise that

He doesn't only want to provide for my life in eternity but also sees and wants to provide for my needs today—mentally, physically, spiritually, and emotionally. I can ask for help because He is able, and He loves me.

Chapter 7

WHEN YOUR MIND NEEDS REST

*Scripture-Based and Science-Backed
Truth to Still Your Restless Thoughts*

YOU WOULD NEVER KNOW IT WAS A PUBLIC BEACH. WE WERE THE ONLY SOULS in sight. I still can't remember exactly how we heard about it when we first moved from Oklahoma to Los Angeles, but I'll never forget the little wooden-planked path, almost hidden, that wound between gorgeous mansions in Malibu, California, leading all the way down to the most beautiful shoreline you can imagine.

That beach was a happy place for my family during the two years we lived in California. We'd bring friends and family who came to visit to our hidden beach. We'd promise as we parked and led our guests down the secret boardwalk that we *did* have permission to be there. Anyone who could find it

119

could enjoy it. We were some of the lucky few who knew about this hidden gem.

It wasn't the type of beach where you could park close and wheel a wagon filled with chairs or umbrellas all the way down to the water, even though we did enjoy those sorts of beaches while we lived in California. The path that led to this practically private stretch of sand was just big enough to walk single file, carrying at most a picnic basket on the long trek from the car to the shore. But let me tell you, that walk was worth it. I can still hear the waves and can picture the way the sunset threw rosy hues across the water and sand.

I think I'll always remember our first trip to that beach on a December evening weeks after we arrived in California—when the water was just warm enough for little children from Oklahoma to run into and splash. The sun set faster than we anticipated, and it seemed as if we were a world away from everything and everyone we had left behind.

When we arrived in December 2017, we didn't know that just two years later the Lord would move us to Franklin, Tennessee. We didn't know our time on the West Coast would be so short. We didn't know that just a few weeks after we arrived in Tennessee, the entire world would shut down with illness. There was so much we didn't know when we set out from Oklahoma, following God's prompting and trusting Him to guide us. But He saw it all. He saw the joy that was waiting for us, and He saw the painful parts of the path where He'd hold us close.

The truth is, that season of our life in California was filled with hard things we didn't see coming. We needed God there in ways we hadn't in Oklahoma. In those two years, we went through so much. My family experienced a health emergency. We walked someone very close to us through a mental health crisis. We navigated financial uncertainty. Our marriage struggled. My heart wasn't in a peaceful place. We dealt with the effects of our own mental and emotional overwhelm. But at the very same time, I was confident that we were exactly where we needed to be, and I was just as sure that I needed the Lord to help me daily.

The contrast of how hard that season was with how many incredible things happened while we were there is really remarkable. We enjoyed so many new experiences. We were able to work with the Christian entertainment industry. We were a part of some powerful church conferences. Our business thrived, and we enjoyed new creative ventures. We made lifelong friends in that season. Nearly every day, we woke up to the sun shining and weather that felt like we were on vacation. We had that beautiful beach and incredible sunsets and so much to explore and enjoy. But there was also so much deep pain. I think sometimes we forget that both can be true at once.

Life can be both beautiful and heavy. Full of sorrow and joy. Full of hope and discouragement just breaths apart, and sometimes held within the same heart,

> **LIFE CAN BE BOTH BEAUTIFUL AND HEAVY. FULL OF SORROW AND JOY.**

mind, and body simultaneously. One does not mean the absence of the other. I'm sure you have experienced this.

Those highs and lows defined our two years in Los Angeles. My mind wondered constantly about the future and thought back over all we had left behind. It was as if my thoughts were in a tug-of-war between what I knew to be true of the Lord meeting us in the current moment and the fear of the future and the pain over what we had left in the past. Do you know what that's like?

The mind of a momma rarely seems to occupy the present moment. Her thoughts are seldom fully in the same room that holds her feet. We do our best to think two steps ahead— planning, problem-solving, peering into tomorrow, hoping that when it comes it will be easier than today. And often, we spend just as much time replaying the past, reviewing all we have done and rehearsing how things could be different now if we had just thought of _____ back then.

Do your thoughts ever race down trails of all the possible outcomes, hoping to come up with a solution that shifts your circumstances? Do your thoughts ever get sucked back in time until you wonder: *If only . . . ?*

How are we ever supposed to rest our minds when they are full not only of what must be done today but also of fear or worry or grief or regret? How are we supposed to experience mental rest when our thoughts race relentlessly?

Is your mind tired, too, friend? Honestly, I'd be shocked if you said, "Actually, no. I'm good. All clear here." Moms are often physically busy, but a mother's mind is what never seems to stop. It keeps track of it all. All the information, all the feelings, all the memories, all the possibilities—good, bad, and uncertain.

Telling a mom that she can rest her mind feels almost as impossible as telling a mom that she can rest her body. Yet we need to rest both. The health of our minds is just as important as the health of our bodies. I don't need to tell you that either, do I? Once again, just like the issue with resting your body isn't whether it's good for you, but rather how to find time to do it; the issue with resting your mind is not *if* it's important but *how* to find moments to give your brain a break. How do we stop overthinking? How do we stop worrying? How do we grab hold of those racing thoughts?

Isaiah 26:3 gives us a hint: "You will keep in perfect peace all who trust in you, all whose thoughts are fixed on you!" (NLT). Life is loud and shouts for our attention. Yet Scripture is clear: We fix our thoughts on Jesus, and He keeps us in peace. It sounds simple, but what does it actually mean? I can hear the Lord speaking to us over all the chaos, kindly helping our hearts to focus: *Eyes on Me, baby girl. Eyes on Me.*

SCIENCE AND SCRIPTURE AGREE ON THIS

Scripture has much to say about the mind. To the church in Philippi, Paul wrote, "Whatever is true, whatever is noble, whatever is right, whatever is pure, whatever is lovely, whatever is admirable—if anything is excellent or praiseworthy—think about such things" (Philippians 4:8).

To the Colossian church, Paul wrote, "Set your minds on things above, not on earthly things" (Colossians 3:2). Nice! I'd love to only think about lovely and pure things, but I do still have to think about dinner and whether that check has been processed and when the doctor's office is going to call me back. I do have to think about whether I have time to thaw the frozen meat so we can eat before our evening events. My mind is full, just like my calendar.

Also, I don't know about you, but my mind doesn't always go to lovely and admirable first. My mind can be grumbly and argumentative, consumed with my problems or pain, focused on fixing my frustrations, planning how to create peace in my own strength, and purposing how to achieve my own plans. My thoughts can be so earthly focused that I forget heavenly truth.

I think that's the point Paul was making. Most of us have spent our lives practicing the present rather than practicing His presence. Day after day we think about what is right in front of us rather than the One who makes His home within us. But there is a way to fix it. There's a way to train our minds to be focused on the eternal while our days are filled with the temporary, and both science and Scripture confirm the process.

THE MORE WE INTENTIONALLY FOCUS ON WHAT IS GOOD AND TRUE, THE MORE NATURAL IT WILL BECOME TO THINK ON THINGS FROM ABOVE.

The more we intentionally focus on what is good and true, the more natural it will become to think on things from above.

Paul wrote, "Be transformed by the renewing of your mind" (Romans 12:2). Thousands of years after Paul wrote these letters, modern scientists now understand the power of the mind to transform the brain. I love when science proves what God has already said.

Here's how it works. Your brain creates connections between brain cells as you perceive the world around you and take in information. These connections are called neural pathways, and they are somewhat like roads down which your thoughts travel. When you're a baby, they start out simple, and as you repeat a process or rehearse an idea in your mind, these connections strengthen, and the neural pathways become more prominent. The more you think a certain thought, the easier it is to think that same thought again.

Scientists used to believe that at a certain age, neural pathways stopped forming. Now researchers understand the brain has the ability to keep changing—so we can keep creating new neural pathways as we intentionally think new thoughts. As you change your thinking, you can change your brain, and as Dr. Daniel Amen, double board-certified psychiatrist, clinical neuroscientist, and *New York Times* bestselling author teaches, if you can change your brain, you can change your life.[1]

If our thoughts change the way our brains are formed, then it makes sense why the apostle Paul urged us to focus on what is true, noble, right, pure, lovely, admirable, excellent, and praiseworthy. Each of these healthy thoughts creates new connections or supports connections already in place. As we meditate on God's Word, our spirits are strengthened, and so are our neural pathways.

In the same way, however, when we worry or replay the past or rehearse our fears of the future, those unhealthy thoughts form paths too. And just like with healthy thoughts, the more we think negatively, the stronger those neural pathways grow, and the easier it becomes to *keep* thinking those negative thoughts.

One study discovered that "brooding too much on negative events is the biggest predictor of depression and anxiety and determines the level of stress people experience."[2] Our brains are highly sophisticated, beautifully intricate machines. If you program your brain to think a certain way, don't be surprised when it does.

My friend, changing our minds about our experiences requires intentionality (and sometimes the help of a trained professional). Please don't think that I'm telling you to just stop thinking about the pain of the past, the mess of this moment, or the fear of the future. Avoiding thoughts about certain aspects of life can be just as damaging as focusing on them. I'm simply reminding you that you are the only one who can decide which neural pathways to strengthen. You can choose to remind yourself of God's promised presence and all He has already done for you. Like the psalmist declared, "I will consider all your works and meditate on all your mighty deeds" (77:12).

FIXING OUR THOUGHTS ON WHAT IS TRUE

When God's people were traveling through the wilderness, God provided for them supernaturally. We discussed previously how He gave them food. He also provided water, direction, and the promise of His presence. Yet they grumbled. They focused on all that was wrong.

God's people had physical freedom, but their minds were still captive to their old ways of thinking. They had to learn to think new thoughts about who God was and how He would take care of them.

In order to help them remember, the Lord instructed them to keep a special jar of the supernatural food He had provided them to eat in the wilderness. He said, "Two quarts of it are to be preserved throughout your generations, so that they may see the bread I fed you in the wilderness when I brought you out of the land of Egypt" (Exodus 16:32 CSB). The quarts were long-lasting evidence of what He had done. He brought His people into physical freedom and then taught them how to stay focused on what was good and what He had accomplished. He gave them reminders to retrain their attention.

In the same way, sometimes we get stuck in old ways of thinking even after we have given our hearts to Jesus. Yet Scripture says, "We have the mind of Christ" (1 Corinthians 2:16). So while we might have a natural bent to wonder why God hasn't answered a prayer or provided a resolution yet, we can shift our focus and remember what God has *already* done for us. We can remember times when He provided, gave us His peace, and kindly showed us what to do next. We can remember the moments when we were certain He held us or sent help or gave us soul rest. We can fix our eyes on the love Jesus revealed on the cross.

As we work to retrain our thoughts, there will be moments when we inevitably replay the pain. But Paul reminded us, "We demolish arguments and every pretension that sets itself up against the knowledge of God, and we take captive every thought to make it obedient to Christ" (2 Corinthians 10:5). When unhealthy thoughts begin, we can arrest them and replace them with what the Word of God says is true.

- **When we feel as if life will always be the way it is right now . . .** we can retrain our minds to remember: "The steadfast love of the LORD never ceases; his mercies never come to an end; they are new every morning; great is your faithfulness" (Lamentations 3:22–23 ESV).
- **When we fear what tomorrow will hold and we begin to rehearse all the possibilities . . .** we can remember Jesus said: "Who of you by worrying can add a single hour to your life?" (Luke 12:25). "Your Father knows what you need before you ask him" (Matthew 6:8).
- **When we doubt our abilities . . .** we can remember that the Lord doesn't expect us to carry the load on our own. He said, "My grace is sufficient for you, for

my power is made perfect in weakness" (2 Corinthians 12:9).

- **When we begin to feel shame or guilt** . . . we can hold on to the promise that "God did not send his Son into the world to condemn the world, but to save the world through him" (John 3:17). And: "Therefore, there is now no condemnation for those who are in Christ Jesus" (Romans 8:1).

- **When we convince ourselves we are all alone** . . . we can remember the Lord never leaves us: "Be strong and courageous. Do not be afraid or terrified because of them, for the LORD your God goes with you; he will never leave you nor forsake you" (Deuteronomy 31:6).

- **When we are certain that no one understands** . . . we can remember Jesus experienced what it meant to be human, and remember He understands. "For we do not have a high priest who is unable to sympathize with our weaknesses, but one who in every respect has been tempted as we are, yet without sin" (Hebrews 4:15 ESV).

- **When we experience suffering** . . . we can consider the words of the psalmist, who said, "My comfort in my suffering is this: Your promise preserves my life" (119:50).

WHAT HOLDS YOUR ATTENTION MATTERS. WHAT YOU SPEND YOUR TIME THINKING ABOUT MATTERS.

What holds your attention matters. What you spend your time thinking about matters. Again I hear the Lord reminding us, *Eyes on Me, baby girl. Eyes on Me.*

FOLLOW THE TRAIL OF HIS PRESENCE

Until recently, I would have called our time in California a "not so good" season. I've noticed that people tend to call seasons "good" when the joy outweighs the sorrow. Likewise, they call seasons "bad" when the pain outweighs the peace. The thing is, the older I get, the more I realize that life is full of hard and heavy in just about every season. Yet we still have the ability to adjust where we fix our focus and in doing so shift our outlooks before our circumstances change.

Just a few weeks ago, my mom and I were looking at old photos and videos together from my family's time in California. I showed her a picture on my phone from that beach in Malibu, and we came across a clip of my oldest son, now in high school, back when he was in second grade. He wore a bright orange shirt and held a little crab in his hands. "Look! A crab!" he said as he proudly showed the camera. His brother and sister gathered around as he continued to present it to them. "It has a mouth!" he said. "And three legs on this side and only two on that side!" They all giggled as he smiled big. He was so proud of himself for holding it.

It was such a simple memory during a really complicated time. I looked up from my phone at my mom and silently replayed the rest of that day. I remembered the heartache and fear. I remembered the anxiety and overwhelm. The unanswered questions. The not-so-good moments were still too intertwined with the good for me to see that video of my kids and not think about the chronic stress behind the scenes.

"It wasn't *all* bad," my mom encouraged, recognizing the expression on my face. She knew all that season had held. She knew all the hardest parts that had come to my mind in that moment. I wanted to argue with her. I wanted to tell her how the pain had outweighed the peace. I wanted to say out loud what I had rehearsed over and over in my mind about that season. It was so easy for my mind to follow the trails of my old thoughts.

I looked back down at my phone. I had a choice. Would I let all my memories of that time, when God had met us so powerfully, be shaded by that dull, achy gray of heartache? Would I call the entire season *bad* because the pain outweighed the peace?

What about you? Is something so heavy on your heart right now that the balance from joy to discouragement seems to be tipping? Is this *entire season* bad? Was that *entire time* when your heart ached a season without God's presence? Or is it possible that there is some good you can store up from those days—a reminder that God has not abandoned you and did not leave you even there?

I believe the Enemy of our hearts would have us write off entire chunks of our story. "Nothing good to remember there!" he lies, pointing out all the pain, hoping we'll take the bait and fix our thoughts on what went wrong.

But the Lord reminds us, *Even there, I was with you. Even there, I was good. Even there, you were safely held. Fix your eyes on Me. Look again and see where I was in that season. Look again and see how I offered My peace. Look again and see how I loved you, strengthened you, comforted you through it. Look again and pull from among the dirt the provision I made possible.*

I looked back down at the photo of the little boy on the beach, beaming with joy as he held the small crab. Then I made a choice to retrain my brain and prayed that my heart would follow.

What a gift for the Lord to give us a chance to trust Him in that season.

What a gift for the Lord to give us the opportunity to rely on His peace.

What a gift to know Him as our supernatural strength.

What a gift to feel His presence when it seemed as though we were on our own.

What a gift to say we had followed Him.

What a gift to know Him as Provider.

What a gift to know Him as Comforter.

What a gift to know Him as Helper.

I followed the trail of His presence in my mind, just as I had followed the narrow walkway down to the beach—and in the process, my brain created a new path for truth-filled thoughts to flow.

YOU ARE THE ONLY ONE

WHO CAN DECIDE WHICH

NEURAL PATHWAYS TO

STRENGTHEN . . . CHOOSE

TO REMIND YOURSELF

OF GOD'S PROMISED

PRESENCE AND ALL HE HAS

ALREADY DONE FOR YOU.

Let's practice shifting our thinking. With minds that naturally bend away from lovely, it can be so much easier to notice the hard and heavy. But when did the Lord come through for you? We've talked extensively about the deep needs you may have in this season of exhaustion, but what good things can you focus on in this moment, even before the season changes? What truth can you stand on right here? What blessings can you put in your jar of remembrance right now?

Peace in our minds doesn't only come when the fear lifts or the worry ceases or the grief is eased. Peace in our thoughts doesn't only come after the heartache yields to hope. Jesus is the Prince of Peace, and we can praise Him even now as we remember, "You will keep in perfect peace all who trust in you, all whose thoughts are fixed on you!" (Isaiah 26:3 NLT). Shift your attention, my friend. Fix your eyes on Him. Rest your mind as you remember peace is right here in the room.

And He's saying, *Eyes on Me, baby girl. Eyes on Me.*

LET'S PRAY

Lord, we know how we have trained our thinking in the past. We know the easy roads our thoughts race down, and they aren't all good or full of truth. So we ask You to bring healing to our brains and refreshment to our thoughts. We ask You to perform a supernatural work and shift the circuitry in how our brains operate; renew our minds as You shift our neural path-

ways away from all that is untrue. Help us have good, healthy, truth-filled thoughts centered on Your Word. Help our minds stay fixed on You. We ask in Jesus's name, amen.

Scriptures to Pray When Your Mind Needs Rest

- "I will consider all your works and meditate on all your mighty deeds" (Psalm 77:12).
- "Let us run with perseverance the race marked out for us, fixing our eyes on Jesus, the pioneer and perfecter of our faith" (Hebrews 12:1–2).
- "May these words of my mouth and this meditation of my heart be pleasing in your sight, LORD, my Rock and my Redeemer" (Psalm 19:14).

Rest in This Truth

I have the mind of Christ. He gives me access to His thoughts, so I will listen for what He says about the situation I'm facing. I will take captive the thoughts that create unhealthy patterns in my mind and subsequently in my actions. He will help me, so I will be transformed by the renewing of my mind.

Chapter 8

WHEN YOU NEED CALMING CONNECTION

The Healing Power of Resting in God's Presence

QUIET VOICES AND THE HUM OF MEDICAL MACHINES WERE THE ONLY SOUNDS JARED and I heard as we walked down the dimly lit hospital hall toward our newborn daughter's incubator. She had been a patient in the neonatal intensive care unit (NICU) for a couple of days, and we hoped this day might be the one when we could finally hold her. This wasn't how we had anticipated spending the first few days after her birth. I'm sure every parent whose child has been in the NICU would agree. We had different plans, but when the doctors said our baby needed immediate help, we were grateful the support was available.

The nurse came into the room and greeted us with a smile. "She's doing really well," she encouraged us, opening the clear box and rearranging the many cords attached to our daughter's tiny body. "Would you like to hold her?" she offered. Keeping our voices down so as to not disturb the other tiny patients, we both exclaimed a hushed, "Yes!" I added, "We had been hoping we might be able to!"

The nurse slowly prepared our daughter's little body to be moved from her warm bed. As she did, she explained something called kangaroo care (or skin-to-skin care), a practice in which a diapered baby is placed on their parent's bare chest. The connection with mom or dad helps the baby regulate their heartbeat, breathing, and body temperature.

I looked over at my husband. I had held our daughter for quite awhile in the delivery room before she was taken to the NICU, but Jared hadn't gotten the same opportunity. "You should hold her," I encouraged him. He removed his shirt and wrapped a blanket around his shoulders and arms, and I watched with so much joy as the nurse carefully placed our little girl on her daddy's chest. He held her safely to his heart. She had been sleeping for much of the time we had been with her, but as she heard her daddy's heartbeat, she opened her eyes, blinking wide with wonder at the new world around her. She hadn't yet been to our house, but she was home in the arms of her father.

Across this world, from palaces to park benches, in the beating chest of every person on this planet drums a driving desire to find our way home, back into the arms of our heavenly Father. We seek connection, longing for and looking for the rest we can experience only when near the Father's chest, tucked safely in His arms. This is what we were created for: connection with God.

The moment you asked Jesus to become the Lord of your life, you received a gift of living as one of His children. No longer estranged, no longer unable to come close because of sin's separation, you now live with unlimited access to the Father who made you just to love you. If you've read this far already and haven't just skimmed ahead to this page, you know what Jesus has done for you. We discussed how He has made Himself available to you. The question that remains is this: Do you live as though you're connected to God with every breath you take? (Most of us, if answering honestly, reply with a no.)

I don't always wake up thinking about God's presence. Even though I know the importance of fixing my thoughts on the Lord, He is not the first thought that comes to my mind every day. Most often, I wake up wondering: *Did I oversleep? Are we going to be late? What important notifications are waiting for me on my phone?*

Like most moms, from the moment I open my eyes, many things demand my attention. I know my day will be full. I know I will be overextended. I know I will need the Lord to help me through all of it. I bet that's mostly true for you too. Here's the thing: We may have found our way back into the loving arms of Jesus when we accepted Him as Savior, but how do we stay connected with Him to receive His rest?

One of my favorite Bible teachers, A. W. Tozer, said in his book *The Purpose of Man*, "The average Christian's life is cluttered with all sorts of activities. We have more going on than we can keep up and still maintain our inner life with God . . . We find ourselves rushing through the devotional aspects of our life to give predominance to mere activities."[1] I believe this has become even truer in the seventy-plus years since Tozer penned this timeless observation.

He didn't just describe a modern problem. He described the tension that has plagued the heart of the busy woman for thousands of years. We are desperate for Him, yet everything else often feels more urgent than time intentionally spent in His presence.

WHAT ARE YOU DESPERATE FOR?

In the book of Luke, we find a familiar story of two sisters, Mary and Martha, who were dear friends of Jesus. You probably know their story, but just in case it has been a while since you read about them in Luke 10, I'll summarize.

Jesus came to His friend Martha's home and began to teach those who gathered there. He had brought a crowd with

Him, and Martha took care of her guests while Mary, Martha's sister, sat at Jesus's feet and listened.

I don't know about you, but there have been plenty of times in my life when I have looked up from what felt like a task that should have been a family project and, rather than notice all the ways others *were* helping, I noticed all the ways they *could* be helping.

I've noticed the overflowing trash cans in the kitchen and the pile of shoes by the front door and wondered why everyone who lives in my house isn't as bothered by the work I see needs to be done. Don't get me wrong or reach out to say that my kids should help with chores; they do. My husband and I are partners in our home and share the workload. Our kids contribute to taking care of what needs to be done around the house. They have responsibilities both for their own spaces and belongings and for the shared spaces and chores. Still, some days I feel like the one who directs all the *doing*. And it makes me feel jealous, frustrated, and all sorts of other emotions that aren't fruits produced by the Spirit of God when my family isn't as flustered as I am by the unfinished work. I feel somewhat abandoned to carry the mental load of all that needs to be done on my own.

So I understand Martha's frustration when she came to Jesus with her heart. I can hear that pain of being left to carry the burden alone when she said, "Lord, don't you care that my sister has left me to do the work by myself?" (v. 40). I wonder if she thought, *Mary clearly doesn't care enough to help, but You*

see me, Jesus. You see she's abandoned me to do this by myself.
You care. Don't You?

And in complete kindness, when Jesus heard Martha's words, He didn't reply with the answer she wanted but the one she needed: "My dear Martha, you are worried and upset over all these details! There is only one thing worth being concerned about. Mary has discovered it, and it will not be taken away from her" (vv. 41–42 NLT).

I love how Jesus didn't exactly say, "Mary is right, Martha. Stop being fussy." He didn't take Mary's side. He didn't rebuke Martha. He lovingly acknowledged how Martha felt. He told her that He knew she was worried and upset, and then He gently revealed the better way.

Jesus acknowledged there's something worth being concerned about, but it's not the work that needs to get done or the people we expect to jump up and join us. It's staying connected to the One who has come close.

I used to think we should aim to be like Mary, only ever sitting at Jesus's feet and learning. Here's the problem with that idea. The work *does* still need to be done. I don't believe Jesus was telling Martha to ignore her guests. Jesus was not saying that what we do for others is unimportant. He was also not saying we shouldn't ask for help when we need it. I believe that Jesus *was* saying the *most* important thing should not be sacrificed even for other important things. Once the most important thing—being with the Lord and spending time in His presence—is discovered, He won't be the One to take it away from us.

I wonder: Are we more desperate to finish our work, or are we more desperate to find our way back to His feet? Really stop to consider it. Because only one brings the deep rest our hearts crave.

> ARE WE MORE DESPERATE TO FINISH OUR WORK, OR ARE WE MORE DESPERATE TO FIND OUR WAY BACK TO HIS FEET?

Do you chase *finished*? Do you just want everything to be done so you can finally relax? I often pray, "Lord, help me figure this out, get this done, carry this load. Please help me find the answers I need and the peace I need. Help me with this problem or that problem." I ask Jesus to help me with whatever it is that I need help doing at that time. This is a good prayer. It's good to believe He wants to help us accomplish whatever needs to be done. But I don't always pray with the same level of desperation in the middle of my day, "Lord, help me remain connected to Your presence even as the work is done. Help me to rest in You even before I have the chance to pause. Help me live with rest in my heart."

My friend, I don't live at your house. I don't know the details of your circumstances. I can't tell you how to organize your schedule or what keeps you rushing from one situation to the next. I do have a feeling that it's a lot. You know you need to spend time with Jesus, but you also know you need to spend time doing everything else as well. You have to take care of your family and your finances and your home, and maybe if there is any leftover time, pay attention to your friendships. There's only so much of you! There's only so much time! You are the definition of *spread too thin*.

And when you finally find a small pocket of time, spending it with Jesus is likely not the first idea that comes to your mind. Can I be *that* honest for a minute? If you're like me, when you feel stressed or pushed or like you never have the opportunity to rest your constantly busy mind and body, you don't think, *If only I could get alone with my Bible and read and pray . . .*

Instead, perhaps you pick up your phone or turn on the TV or even do healthy things like walk or garden or play pickleball. All the while, you still desperately need the peace and rest that can only be found as you stay connected to the Lord.

So let me remind us both of this very important truth: God meets us wherever we are. He is always available. You don't have to be in a quiet closet or in a special spot to lean into His presence and connect with His Spirit. Altars don't always look like wooden railings at the front of churches. They aren't always found in a sanctuary (even though they often are).

Altars can look like a sink full of dirty dishes, a quiet bedroom, a messy desk, or a moving car. We carry our altars wherever we go . . . continually sacrificing our own wills and time and expectations for the good, good plans of our Father.

We bend our hearts even while we busy our hands and remind ourselves that Jesus's sacrifice wasn't just for eternity. It was so we could rest in the assurance of His presence each moment leading up to it.

How do we cling daily to the promise of God with us? How do we live connected to the heart of God all day long? I suppose we have to first remember that He's not passing us by but has come to remain with us.

TOUCH-AND-STAY JESUS

We don't know much about the woman found in Luke 8 who had bled for over twelve years, but we do know that just one touch of the edge of Jesus's robe changed her life.

This woman had a physical illness no one else could heal, and it separated her from everyone she may have loved. The religious law was clear about who could and couldn't come close to her. But she had heard about a healer named Jesus. Desperate, and prepared for whatever consequence would come from being in a crowd, she was determined to grab the hem of Jesus's robe as He passed by, believing He could heal her. As she did, the Lord stopped and acknowledged her touch. Power had left Him. He turned and spoke to her, "Daughter, your faith has healed you. Go in peace" (v. 48). In that instant, she found both healing for her body and hope for her heart. All it took was one touch.

Over and over throughout Scripture, we see that just a moment in the presence of Jesus can change a person's life. But I bring up this one woman's story to remind us that we have access beyond the corner of Jesus's cloak. Yes, one touch does change everything, but we don't have a touch-and-go relationship with the Lord. We have access to the inner chamber of

WE DON'T HAVE A
TOUCH-AND-GO
RELATIONSHIP WITH THE
LORD. WE HAVE ACCESS
TO THE INNER CHAMBER
OF GOD'S HEART.

God's heart. He is not walking away from you, strolling on to help others and offering you only a brief opportunity to brush your fingertips across His fringe.

Paul explained to us in Romans 8:15–16, "You received God's Spirit when he adopted you as his own children. Now we call him, 'Abba, Father.' For his Spirit joins with our spirit to affirm that we are God's children" (NLT). The Holy Spirit has joined with your spirit and stays with you. He reveals Jesus to you.

In John 14:16, Jesus said, "I will ask the Father, and he will give you another Advocate, who will never leave you" (NLT). That's pretty clear. The Advocate, the Holy Spirit, doesn't come and go, popping in and out of our lives.

Jesus said, "He is the Holy Spirit, who leads into all truth. The world cannot receive him, because it isn't looking for him and doesn't recognize him. But you know him, because he lives with you now and later will be in you. No, I will not abandon you as orphans—I will come to you" (John 14:17–18 NLT). He went on to say, "Peace I leave with you; my peace I give you" (v. 27). And He has. He made a way to be with us always through the presence of the Holy Spirit. This Comforter is with you now as you read these words. He has been with you all day. He will be with you as you close these pages. He brings peace and wisdom. He reminds you of what the Word of God says is true. He reveals Jesus to *you*.

Jesus said to the woman with the issue of blood, "Go in peace," and she returned to her life as He walked away. But Jesus says to you now, "I will not abandon you." If just one touch from the Lord can change our lives, how much more will every part of our lives be changed by continual access to the Spirit of God every moment of every day? The truth is, we have the access to the Holy Spirit, but often we lack the awareness of His presence.

I can almost hear you wondering, *Okay, so, how do I shift my attention? How do I stay connected, living as though He is near?* The same way we shift our attention for anyone else in our lives. We turn our hearts toward them, and we listen when they speak.

COMMUNICATING WITH THE COMFORTER

"Mom? Earth to Mom? Can you even hear me? Where are you?"

I was sitting on the floor of my living room, still in my bathrobe, directing traffic as my three kids got ready for school. I was helping one with their hair and the other find a water bottle. I was signing permission slips and passing out cash for an upcoming field trip. The previous thirty minutes had been a lot. The previous few weeks had been a lot, and honestly, the overwhelm of the morning had finally convinced my body that I wasn't okay. This time, rather than panic, I had disconnected, and I felt like I was asleep with my eyes open. I was going through all the necessary motions, but my mind was a million miles away. I had tuned everyone out.

"Can you even hear me?" my oldest son asked again.

"Sorry," I apologized. "I was just thinking about something else." He didn't have my attention. He knew it and I knew it. "What were you saying?"

He sighed, and I knew it carried more than frustration for simply that morning. I hadn't been myself since my hysterectomy. My brain was foggy. My energy was gone. My focus was nearly nonexistent. My son's comment revealed a bigger issue than just a morning of distraction. My family needed me to tune in to them, so that's exactly what I worked to do. I focused for the rest of that morning, and then, as I made efforts to seek healing for my mind and body, I also intentionally made changes to my schedule to make sure my kids and I had the chance to connect every day.

Knowing most of our daytime hours would be busy for the next few months, every night before bed, I'd go into my oldest son's room and pull out his desk chair next to his bed. I'd listen as he talked about his day. He needed to know I valued time alone with him, and I wanted to hear about what mattered most in his life. He'd tell me funny stories about his friends and concerns about the future. We talked about the big stuff and the stuff that felt big to him. It all mattered. And I started to notice a change in how we interacted throughout the day as a result of those intentional one-on-one moments together.

What started with my oldest continued with my other two children. One by one, I made my way through my kids' bedrooms every night, stopping and listening and asking and listening and laughing and listening. Listening is so important.

When my kids were tiny, I'd look forward to bedtime for an entirely different reason. Bedtime meant I was off duty (well, until someone woke up and I was back on duty). Now, these nighttime talks with my teenagers and my preteen are my favorite time of day, not because it signals the end of my day but because it's when I can easily give them my full attention. During these talks, my face turned toward them tells them I see them and hear their hearts.

Connection requires communication, and to grow relationally with the ones we care about, including the Lord, we have to make space to grow conversationally as well. Truthfully, communication is the vehicle that carries connection between people, and I have always found it fascinating.

When I was in college, before I received a degree in biblical studies, I pursued a degree in organizational/interpersonal communications. One of the most interesting lessons from those classes I took in the early 2000s explored a theory called SIP, or social information processing. SIP explores how communicating via electronic means may influence the relationships we have with the people we know only through these computer-mediated communications. My professor made a point during one lecture on SIP that I still think of often.

CONNECTION REQUIRES

COMMUNICATION, AND TO

GROW RELATIONALLY WITH

THE ONES WE CARE ABOUT,

INCLUDING THE LORD, WE

HAVE TO MAKE SPACE TO

GROW CONVERSATIONALLY

AS WELL.

She explained that when we stand in front of one another, communicating face-to-face, we gulp information. We take in the other person's expressions and posture, perceiving even the slightest nuance of tone and temperament. Whereas online, we take in one another in the smallest samples . . . a *SIP* of communication at a time, if you will. What a properly named theory.

I have to wonder, when it comes to communication with the Lord, do you feel like you interact with Him in sips or gulps? I'm obviously not asking if you speak to Him through a computer. I'm asking if you feel like He's on the other side of the universe rather than standing in the room with you when He speaks. Do you read the Bible remembering that the Holy Spirit is revealing the meaning of those words to your heart from the position of being joined with your spirit? Or do you read it as though it is a letter written and sent across time from the One who *was* rather than the One who *does* make His home in your heart?

What about when you pray? Do you pray like you're sending an email or a text out into the unknown, hopefully received and opened but not always clearly answered? Or do you pray like you're talking to your heavenly Father, whose Son paid the highest price to make it possible for Him to walk right into the room and chat about your day?

Friend, the Lord did not design us for sips of His Spirit but for submersion into all He is, baptizing us into communion with Himself. You have His full attention. He sees you.

FRIEND, THE LORD DID NOT DESIGN US FOR SIPS OF HIS SPIRIT BUT FOR SUBMERSION INTO ALL HE IS.

He hears you. He is speaking right back to you. We were made for communion with Him, and communion requires communication.

Yet life can be so loud, can't it? The truth is, while we can connect with the Lord anywhere, sometimes we have to break away and get quiet to hear what's on God's heart. I think that is exactly why Jesus would take time to retreat to quiet places to be alone and speak to His Father.

Mark 1:35 records, "Very early in the morning, while it was still dark, Jesus got up, left the house and went off to a solitary place, where he prayed." This wasn't a singular event. Luke 5:16 tells us, "Jesus often withdrew to lonely places and prayed." If the Son of God in human flesh needed time alone with His Father, how much more do we?

Jesus said in the Sermon on the Mount, "When you pray, go into your room, and when you have shut your door, pray to your Father who is in the secret place; and your Father who sees in secret will reward you openly" (Matthew 6:6 NKJV). Jesus did not mean we should not pray openly. Jesus prayed publicly on multiple occasions. In John 11:41–42, Jesus called out to His Father, "Father, I thank you that you have heard me. I knew that you always hear me, but I said this for the benefit of the people standing here, that they may believe that you sent me." Praying publicly is a great way to speak to the Lord. We can hear from God and speak to God while we're on the go, taking care of those we love, working, running errands. There's no limit to when and where we can pray . . . and yet Jesus also made the point to tell us to find time to be alone with our heavenly Father, to go into our room and speak to Him in private.

Our families reveal the importance of this truth. I can talk to my husband while I look up something on my phone or sort through the mail, yet you had better believe I also need to make time to be alone with him and hear his heart and share mine. I can stand with my back to my kids and cook dinner on the stove while they tell me about the grades they earned on their tests, but at some point in the day, they need me to turn and look them in the eye and say, "I'm here. This matters. What is it you want to tell me?" If life can be so loud that it's not always easy to prioritize connecting with those right in front of us, of course it takes effort to find time to be alone with the Lord.

We can't "just one second, Jesus" our way through all our days, desperate for finished work and never desperate to find moments alone at His feet. Jesus said, "If anyone thirsts, let him come to Me and drink" (John 7:37 NKJV). He's called the fount of living water, yet we merely sip, never pausing long enough to drink deeply from the well that doesn't run dry. Our hearts find rest as we commune with the Lord, and as it turns out, our bodies find rest when we connect with Him too.

OUR HEARTS FIND REST AS WE COMMUNE WITH THE LORD, AND AS IT TURNS OUT, OUR BODIES FIND REST WHEN WE CONNECT WITH HIM TOO.

CO-REGULATING WITH THE CREATOR

When my daughter was young, she hated going to the doctor. Absolutely despised it. It didn't matter if the doctor was simply performing a checkup or my daughter had an ear infection; she fought all the help the doctor and the doctor's staff tried to provide. In her mind, the help the doctor offered didn't outweigh the fear in her heart.

Every appointment, she would cling with all of the strength in her tiny body around my neck. She was sure of one thing: Mommy was safe.

During one particular appointment, tests were needed. It was overwhelming for both of us. I wished there was an easier way. I wished we didn't need them. But they were important. She wasn't happy. So many tears. So much fear. When it was all done, I picked her up and held her safely in my arms.

I sat and held her close while I repeated, "I've got you. You're safe. Mommy has you. It's over, baby. You're okay. You're okay. You're okay." I put one of her ears to my heart and covered the other with my hand. I rocked back and forth and sang it over and over until the calm of my voice and the sound of my heartbeat did what I was sure they could do.

My love conquered her fear.

Her tears slowed. Her tense frame relaxed. And she rested in the peace of my arms.

The scientific world has a name for this. It's called *co-regulation*.

Put simply, "Co-regulation is the process of someone with a regulated nervous system, meaning they are feeling safe and relaxed, effectively sharing their calm with someone whose nervous system is spiraling out of control."[2]

You co-regulated with your child all of those times you held your baby close when they cried. Your own heartbeat, breath, and presence brought peace to your child's developing nervous system. Each time you picked them up, each time you helped them calm down, each time you worked through a meltdown at any age, you were teaching your child how to regulate their bodies under stress. You shared your peace with your children similarly to the way God shares His peace with His.

If science confirms that a calm friend or family member can share their peace with us, how much more can the One called Comforter calm our breathing, still our racing hearts, and reset our nervous systems? His presence can bring regulation to our anxious and overwhelmed bodies just as He brings rest to our weary souls.

Deep breath.

Momma, resting in the presence of the Lord is not a waste of time. It doesn't take away from the important work you do. It's not something to add to your to-do list. No, my friend. Rest is your spiritual inheritance,

> **RESTING IN THE PRESENCE OF THE LORD IS NOT A WASTE OF TIME.**

paid for with the blood of Jesus, accessed through communion with His Spirit, and enjoyed as we speak to and listen for the Lord in the secret place. Rest is healing.

Just as I held my daughter close to my heart until her tense frame relaxed and she was eased by the comfort of my love, we need the greatest Love, the Love that conquered all fear, to wrap us in His arms and whisper, *I've got you. You're safe. You're okay. You're okay. You're okay.* He sees you. He hears you. He's with you. Let's rest in Him and allow the presence of the Comforter to calm our souls, bodies, and minds.

LET'S PRAY

Lord, the psalmist sang, "Return to your rest, my soul, for the LORD has been good to you" (116:7). We understand that everything You have been in the past is a reminder of everything You'll be to us in the future. So we tell our souls to return to the rest You offer. You have brought peace to our bodies when we didn't even know what was happening. Help us stay connected to You all day long. Help us earnestly desire time alone with You. Help us hear You clearly and speak to You directly as a Father who comes close. We ask in Jesus's name, amen.

Scriptures to Pray When You Need Calming Connection

- "My heart says of you, 'Seek his face!' Your face, LORD, I will seek" (Psalm 27:8).
- "Praise be to the God and Father of our Lord Jesus Christ, the Father of compassion and the God of all comfort, who comforts us in all our troubles, so that we can comfort those in any trouble with the comfort we ourselves receive from God" (2 Corinthians 1:3–4).
- "Shout for joy, you heavens; rejoice, you earth; burst into song, you mountains! For the LORD comforts his people and will have compassion on his afflicted ones" (Isaiah 49:13).
- "For you bless the godly, O LORD; you surround them with your shield of love" (Psalm 5:12 NLT).

Rest in This Truth

Jesus gave His life to make it possible for me to find comfort and rest in the presence of God. I have unlimited access to God, so I will find rest and heal as I stay connected to His heart.

Chapter 9

WHEN YOU START TO HEAL

Finding Hope in the Signs That Stress Is Subsiding

LAST FALL, I DROVE FORTY-FIVE MINUTES FROM MY HOUSE IN THE MIDDLE OF Northwest Oklahoma to the nearest Hobby Lobby. If I lived in Luxembourg, I could have reached France, Belgium, and Germany in the same amount of time. Instead, I only made it to Enid, America. I parked my car, walked inside, and went to a section of the store that I cannot remember ever intentionally shopping in prior to that moment. I love Hobby Lobby decor and holiday items, but this trip wasn't for half-off ceramics or ornaments. I was looking for paints, brushes, and a canvas.

There's a huge wall in my dining room that has been empty for the majority of the last two years. Since moving into this house, I haven't been able to decide what I want to hang in that space and look at every day. Not only is this wall one of the first spaces a guest sees when entering my home, but the dining room is part of the combined living area. This wall is visible from the front door, kitchen, living room, and most importantly, the chairs where we sit to eat most of our meals. I felt an unreasonable and unnecessary pressure to select the perfect art for that space, as if whatever I chose could never be changed. This is why that wall has remained bare for the better part of the last two years. I just couldn't make up my mind.

Let me pause this story to assure you that this chapter isn't about artwork or decorating a house. Not really. According to social media, everyone seems to be an expert on those things anyway. No, this chapter is about the hope one overwhelmed momma discovered almost by accident and the promise that signs of healing can show up in the most unexpected places.

Back to the story.

I could not find a piece of art to fill the space that I could afford and would enjoy looking at every day. I had narrowed down the style I liked. I knew the size I wanted. I just couldn't complete a purchase.

So, after years of staring at a blank wall, I found myself standing in the craft store, staring at a wall of paints for the art I had somehow convinced myself I could create for that very important space.

It's funny. I couldn't decide on art to buy for the wall, but I was pretty confident in my amateur abilities to paint something. Now, other than the art classes I took as electives during high school, painting hasn't been a part of my life. But that Saturday afternoon, I was fully convinced that if I just tried, without any professional training other than the guidance of public education and public broadcasting's Bob Ross, I could paint something worth hanging in my home.

I chose paint colors that day purely by preference. Warm rose, deep green, peachy coral, muted blue . . . these, of course, were not their proper names. I didn't even know what I wanted to paint, but I knew the colors I wanted to include. So as I stood there selecting acrylics, brushes, and a palette, I was curious about what would come from this adventure. I was equally curious to see if my attention span would allow me to finish whatever painting I began. My family knows I don't have the greatest record of finishing my spontaneously creative projects. However, what happened the next day surprised just about everyone in my family.

I set up my new wooden, twelve-dollar easel and opened the curtains in my bright home office on that September Sunday that felt almost like autumn. I placed the blank thirty-six-by-forty-eight-inch canvas on the easel and squeezed a selection of favorite paint colors onto my brand-new plastic palette. For the next three hours, I painted.

I do want to pause again here to say that I remember the days of little kids and a husband who worked out of town for months on end, and how I used to dream of spending five minutes alone (even if it was just to use the restroom). I do appreciate how special it was that I got to paint for three hours and that I had the resources to purchase the materials to paint simply because I wanted to.

Back to the story again.

As I began to brush the paint onto the canvas, the strokes revealed a landscape of rolling hills blanketed with thick emerald trees lit by a warm sun rising or setting (viewer's choice) in the distance. And it wasn't half bad. A little abstract . . . but not half bad.

Stroke after stroke, I painted the forest I had walked through in the prior season of my life. Not the physical forest, but the emotional one that had felt like a never-ending maze. I had lived beneath those trees for years, just wanting to find my way to a clearing. I had lived beneath them again even after finding my way out as a guide for other mommas on their journeys.

I knew what the scene looked like from the forest floor. I knew what life was like walking along the root-raised paths. But this season of my life was different, so the perspective of the painting was different also. No longer feeling lost, I painted as if the viewer was looking down on the forest below. The trees didn't look so scary from up there.

I finished in one day and hung my painting on the wall in the dining room once it had dried the next afternoon. And it's perfect not because it's in any way professional or polished, but because art is supposed to have meaning—and that painting is like a memorial to the Lord of what He has safely walked me through. It's a constant reminder that no matter what comes next, I know the view from the clearing. I have made it through the hard and heavy, dimly lit, and lonely forest floor. And I can trust the Lord will lead me through every forest that will follow. I didn't realize it then, but that painting in just about every way was one of the first signs of my healing.

CREATED TO CREATE

When you think of being creative, what comes to your mind? Perhaps because I just mentioned painting, you think of art. Maybe you thought of a crafty woman in your life who is always coming up with projects for her house or homemade treats for her kids' birthday parties. Maybe you thought of a woman who can make something out of nothing, crafting the cutest gifts or decorations for her home. Maybe you thought of a baker or gardener or planner. Maybe you thought of an entrepreneur who is creative with business. Maybe you thought, *I'm creative!*

I know creative nail techs and hairstylists. I know creative chefs and dancers and graphic designers. I know creative landscapers and contractors and DIYers. I know creative doctors and house cleaners. I know creative writers and teachers and bankers and administrative assistants. As *Encyclopedia Britannica* defines it, creativity is "the ability to make or otherwise bring into existence something new, whether a new solution to a problem, a new method or device, or a new artistic object or form."[1]

When God made us in the garden of Eden, He made us in His image, with the ability to be creative as He is. We are introduced to God as Creator in Genesis 1:1, which says, "In the beginning God *created* . . ." He created light. He created the heavens and the earth. He created the sky and the seas. He created land. He created animals to fill the skies and seas and animals to fill the land. And then He created His masterpiece: a man and a woman, formed in His likeness, made from dust, and breathed into animation by His Spirit.

After resting from His creation, God spoke to the man and woman He'd made, directing them to also create, saying, "Be fruitful and multiply" (v. 22 NLT). Notice that the first introduction we have of the Lord is as the Creator, and the first assignment God gave humanity was to create.

Today, we continue to be like Him as we create like Him. We create families and homes. We create routines and rhythms. We create and grow relationships and community. We reflect the nature of God as we create with Him in every area of our lives.

I recently learned, however, that when we become stressed, our brains struggle to operate creatively because they turn their focus toward security. Instead of the prefrontal cortex (the area of the brain that plays a crucial role in attention, planning, working memory, and the expression of emotions) working optimally, stress "can cause a rapid and dramatic loss of prefrontal cognitive abilities."[2] Stress shifts the brain into survival mode, forcing it to function from its more primitive parts. The brain's cognition, understanding, decision-making, and mood are all impacted, and creativity fades as our brains begin operating out of the parts focused on simply keeping safe.[3]

I'm pretty sure this is why it's so stinkin' hard to figure out what to make for dinner at the end of a long, stressful day. It's why we shout the wrong name when hollering for our kids or why we can't easily remember our online passwords. Stress makes memory recall and all those little decisions more difficult, if not impossible. It powers down innovative ideas and creative solutions. (It even explains why I struggled with writer's block for a decent portion of last spring. The stress hit after I got sick, my grandmother went to the hospital, and one of my kids needed to leave public school to be homeschooled in the middle of the semester.) Stress suffocates creativity.

It wasn't ever supposed to be this way. Remember, stress was never supposed to be a part of our stories. God made us with the distinct ability to find *everything* we need in Him. Yet when sin and separation came into the world, it changed how our bodies (including our brains) function. Stress shifts our focus from freedom to fear, from creativity to concern, and from feeling secure in God's protection to continually searching for reassurance that we are safe.

Scripture is clear in John 10:10: "The thief comes only to steal and kill and destroy." He comes to steal our peace and our health. He comes to kill our dreams, relationships, and bodies. He comes to destroy our hopes, plans, and purpose. He comes to bring stress into our stories and shift our focus from who God made us to be. But the second half of John 10:10 offers us a better word, as Jesus said: "I have come that they may have life, and have it to the full."

Everything that was lost in the garden was restored through the cross. We may live with brains that still experience stress, but Jesus offers us peace that brings healing to our hearts, souls, and even our brain function.

I didn't realize the significance of what my painting truly meant that afternoon in September. I didn't know that my brain and nervous system were healing or that I was moving out of simply surviving as the stress subsided. I just knew I had a capacity to create that wasn't there before. It was like I had been holding my breath, and when I could finally breathe again, the exhale was pretty enough to hang on the wall.

SIMPLE SIGNS OF HEALING

I won't assume you're feeling safer or more settled now than you did when you first picked up this book. I hope you do, but I don't know. But I do believe that no matter your current situation, you will look up at some point as your heart begins to heal and realize you aren't where you once were—and I want you to notice, so you can be encouraged when it comes.

It's easy to notice when life gets even a little harder, but rarely do we actually pay attention when life gets *any* easier.

I know this because one day I finished my laundry and didn't notice. I emptied the baskets, folded the clothes, and put them away . . . and treated the accomplishment as if it were part of a regular day. Just a few years before, I could not have imagined ever being so settled that I had the capacity to keep up with the laundry. I understand that this might not be your story. You might be a person who has to have things perfectly in order, especially when you're stressed. But for me, the unfolded laundry was like a monument to what I could not accomplish.

It taunted me, saying, "I'll be here forever. You may work so hard to finally put me away, but I'll be back again tomorrow. Other moms can figure it out. Why can't you?" (Laundry has a lot to say, I guess.) I wore the weight of this unfinished work, disappointed in myself for not being the woman I wanted to be—for not being the woman who knew how to get it all done and the woman who had the mental, emotional, and physical availability to do so. That was the real issue underneath everything else: the disconnect between what I believed I should be able to do and what I actually had the capacity to complete.

But one day, not in some weird spurt of energy or frustrated-cleaning kind of way (do you ever have those?), but in an "I have room in my mind and in my schedule to get it done" sort of way, I was able to finish the laundry. It stayed done. When another load materialized the next day, I washed it. When I got behind, I caught up. I was able to use the methods I had learned previously but hadn't been able to put into practice.

The laundry stopped being the massive mountain (physically and emotionally) it had been for most of my adult life. But here's the thing: As it happened, as I got caught up and stayed caught up, I didn't even notice. There was no personal celebration. It wasn't a recognizable event, like learning to ride a bike. No one had pushed me until I realized I was finally pedaling on my own down the street, able to shout with excited victory, "I'm doing it! I'm doing it!"

It was a silent healing. Life just went on. I did the laundry because I could do the laundry. And I missed the simple sign that my heart, mind, and body were shifting. Like I said, it's easy to notice when life gets harder, but rarely do we pay attention when life gets even a little easier. Mostly because we don't want to take steps *toward* healing; we want to *be* healed. We want to be all the way out of the forest. We want to be in the clearing.

But I wish I had noticed as it was happening. I wish I had recognized that being able to keep up was a sign that maybe, just maybe, my brain was a little healthier than before. Maybe my heart was finally beginning to believe I was safe.

My friend, I don't want you to miss the signs of your healing.

I DON'T WANT YOU TO MISS THE SIGNS OF YOUR HEALING.

Because truthfully, sometimes, the trees all look the same. Not until we make it out the other side do we realize just how close we had been to the clearing all along. But what a gift it would be to see how far you've come in the midst of the journey—to discover you're not where you once were, that the stress is subsiding, and that the healing has begun!

So what are some of the everyday signs that perhaps you're shifting away from the effects of stress? Maybe you fold the laundry. Maybe you paint a painting. Or maybe one day you realize you're breathing deeply again without having to remind yourself to inhale and exhale. Perhaps you will notice you aren't as frustrated with your family as you had been, not as snippy about simple things. You are able to plan and prepare. You might be getting more sleep, or even dreaming about the future again.

Just as a person's brain can operate more creatively when healing from stress and survival, healing can also look like the capacity to do what you *want* to do in addition to what you *have* to do. You might bake or garden or design or spend time redecorating your spaces. You might come up with a creative lesson, craft a creative solution, or prepare an art project for your kids or grandkids.

As the healing unfolds, you may notice you have greater capacity to connect with others, including your spouse, children, friends, family, coworkers, patients, employees, students, or neighbors. Those texts that previously went unanswered— not only because you were too busy to respond but also because you did not have enough energy to think about what you wanted to say—might finally be answered.

You might stop procrastinating. You might make plans and keep them. You might actually want to add to your schedule because you have room in your heart for what those commitments may bring. You might surprise yourself by being spontaneous, or maybe you'll surprise yourself by being prepared.

When our brains begin to heal from the stress, the signs can be so subtle we might miss them. They might not look like a massive painting on the wall, but every bit of healing in our lives is worth noticing and celebrating because Jesus gave His life to pay for *each* part. So while I know it can be painful to be reminded of how far you are from where you might want to be, I believe it is a gift to be able to recognize healing as it comes.

So whether you're thinking, *I see how far I have to go* or you're thinking, *Wow, Jesus has already brought me so much healing* . . . Can I say something that might, perhaps, be a little hard to hear?

AS YOU HEAL, YOU MUST BE NICE TO YOURSELF ON THIS JOURNEY.

As you heal, you must be nice to yourself on this journey. You can't bully yourself better or shame yourself free, hoping that condemnation somehow brings healing. It won't.

You have to forgive yourself for not being more when you were just trying to make it. Perhaps that was years ago, or perhaps that's how you feel right now. You have to stop being so hard on yourself for needing the Lord's help in those (or these) moments. You have to stop being disappointed in yourself when you *know* you did (or are doing) all you can, even if you can see now how it could be better or different.

I think that's one of the most heartbreaking things women do. We don't give ourselves grace for all we have endured or what we're presently walking through, yet no one knows better than we do how hard it is to be us. Clearly struggling and in need of love and support, we are the first to say to ourselves, "Just get over it. Why are you this way? Just push through!"

That's not the way the Lord speaks to us. It's not how He feels about our need for Him. I want you to picture for a moment the Lord in front of you, taking your face in His hands, locking eyes with you, and saying, *Peace.*

Peace over your past.
Peace over your present.
Peace over your future.
Peace over your thoughts.
Peace over your memories.
Peace over your disappointments.
Peace piercing through the shame.
Peace forcing back the fear.
Peace sweeping away the stress.

Deep breath.

Pause and listen for what Jesus wants to say to you right now. He offers us loving-kindness. He doesn't condemn. He doesn't shame. We must not push away the grace Jesus paid for with His blood. My friend, choosing to rest in the grace He offers rather than slathering ourselves in shame is a sign our hearts are healing.

See, there will be signs of your body and mind's healing—but I also believe there are signs when your heart begins to heal as well. You may even feel safe enough to sing.

SONGS OF HEALING

We've talked about the Israelites leaving Egypt, but there's one last part of that story I want to share with you. After safely making their way across the dry ground of the Red Sea floor, with the Egyptians swept away and no longer a threat, Moses and all the Israelites couldn't help but sing praises to the Lord.

> The LORD is my strength and my defense;
> > he has become my salvation.
> He is my God, and I will praise him,
> > my father's God, and I will exalt him.
> The LORD is a warrior;
> > the LORD is his name. (Exodus 15:2–3)

Exodus 15:20–21 goes on to say,

Then Miriam the prophet, Aaron's sister, took a timbrel in her hand, and all the women followed her, with timbrels and dancing. Miriam sang to them:

"Sing to the Lᴏʀᴅ,

    for he is highly exalted.

Both horse and driver

    he has hurled into the sea."

I love that the sound of singing surrounded God's people as they walked out of that traumatic time (still with quite a journey ahead). I love that they felt safe enough to sing. I love that these songs of freedom and worship are the first recorded songs in Scripture. And I love what their songs teach us about praise.

Like David singing in the back of the cave, sometimes there are moments in our lives when we praise the Lord and declare His goodness even before we see it or feel it. In those moments, singing the truth of who God is shifts our hearts, steadies our minds, and even reduces the stress in our bodies. But Moses and Miriam teach us about another kind of song that spills out when our hearts feel safe and we can't help but praise the Lord who held us through all the trouble.

When your heart starts to heal, joy returns. Hope rises. Peace settles. And often our heart's lost song returns.

My friend, healing is coming. The dawn is breaking. There are signs all around that the Prince of Peace is present. You know the truth now to stand on. You know how to lean in and rest in His love.

You will not always be where you are right now, but the Lord will always be just as close as He is in this moment.

He will hold you when life has been a lot and the world feels unsafe. He will hold you when you want to hide, and when all the alarms are sounding. He will go with you and give you rest for your soul, strength for your body, and peace for your mind. He will be with you when you feel discouraged or disconnected and need His calming comfort. And He will hold you as you heal.

Take one last deep breath with me.

Before you held this book in your hands, the Lord saw you. Before you listened to the audiobook or your eyes skimmed across the screen of your tablet, before these words were presented to you in whatever way they have come to you, the Lord saw this exact moment. He knew what would be happening in your day, the stresses you'd face this week, and the situations that are the heaviest on your heart in this season of your life. He knew you would need Him right here, right now.

And in His kindness, He orchestrated all the steps behind the scenes for the last few years, leading to this one, so He could make sure you knew deeply in your heart, no matter what comes,

You are forever safely held by a good God who loves you.

May you continue to lean in and daily discover healing rest in Him.

HEALING IS COMING. THE DAWN IS BREAKING. THERE ARE SIGNS ALL AROUND THAT THE PRINCE OF PEACE IS PRESENT. YOU KNOW THE TRUTH NOW TO STAND ON. YOU KNOW HOW TO LEAN IN AND REST IN HIS LOVE.

LET'S PRAY

Lord, thank You for being the God who heals the hurting heart, the racing mind, and the exhausted body. Thank You for the signs that remind us You are leading us toward wholeness. We thank You for walking us deeper into Your love. We thank You for being the God who has revealed so much hope to our hearts. May we continue to trust that Your grace is sufficient for us. Your strength is made perfect in our weakness. Help us look back and see where You were. Help us look around and see You near. Help us look toward tomorrow and trust You'll meet us there. When the days are long and our hearts are weary, help us lean into Your everlasting arms and trust that we are secure. Thank You, Lord, for holding us close to Your heart and helping us discover healing rest in you. We ask in Jesus's name, amen.

Scriptures to Pray When You Start to Heal

- "Lord my God, I called to you for help, and you healed me" (Psalm 30:2).
- "He brought me out into a spacious place; he rescued me because he delighted in me" (Psalm 18:19).
- "You turned my wailing into dancing; you removed my sackcloth and clothed me with joy, that my heart may sing your praises and not be silent. Lord my God, I will praise you forever" (Psalm 30:11–12).

Rest in This Truth

God is my healer. I've experienced His healing in the past. I will experience His healing in the future. There are signs that my life is shifting and won't always be this stressful, overwhelming, or exhausting. I will listen for the voice of the Lord who speaks hope to my heart, rest for my soul, truth for my mind, and peace to my body. My God is the God who brings healing, and I will rest in Him.

ACKNOWLEDGMENTS

I WOULD LIKE TO ACKNOWLEDGE SOME OF THE MEDICAL PROFESSIONALS WHO have been a part of my journey to discover Healing Rest over the last few years.

To Dr. Andrea McEachern and the team at Reliant Direct Primary Care: Thank you for taking such good care of my family. Thank you for advocating for health in our bodies, minds, and spirits. Dr. McEachern, you have been a trusted guide on my personal journey toward health, and my life has been changed by your wisdom and compassion. Thank you for listening to every concern, searching for answers, and always showing my family that we can trust your sound advice. Your servant heart is a picture of the Lord's kind love for us, and I'm so grateful He brought us into your care.

To Holly Shockley and Blake Imel at Thrive Christian Counseling: Thank you for joining my family on our journey toward healing. In His goodness and love, the Lord brought us to the team He knew we needed. I always say that being found isn't the absence of the forest, but the presence of a guide who knows the way forward. We are grateful to be found by you both. Thank you for meeting us in the middle of our journey and walking with us toward peace, hope, and healing. The healing you have brought to our family will ripple into future generations.

To Dr. Neha Kansara and the team at Amen Clinics: We are so grateful for your whole person approach to mental health treatment. You have been a part of so many answered prayers, and your recommendations have been life-changing in our home. We are so grateful for you.

NOTES

INTRODUCTION

1. Becky Thompson, *Peace: Hope and Healing for the Anxious Momma's Heart* (WaterBrook, 2020), xix.

CHAPTER 1

1. C. S. Lewis, *The Four Loves* (Harcourt Brace & Co., 1960), 78.

CHAPTER 4

1. Olivia Guy-Evans, "Fight, Flight, Freeze, or Fawn: How We Respond to Threats," Simply Psychology, last updated November 9, 2023, https://www.simplypsychology.org/fight -flight-freeze-fawn.html.
2. Brianna Chu et al., "Physiology, Stress Reaction," StatPearls Publishing, last updated May 7, 2024, https://www.ncbi.nlm.nih .gov/books/NBK541120.
3. Amy Arnsten, Carolyn M. Mazure, and Rajita Sinha, "Everyday Stress Can Shut Down the Brain's Chief Command

Center," *Scientific American*, April 1, 2012, https://www
.scientificamerican.com/article/this-is-your-brain-in-meltdown.

4. American Psychological Association, "Stress in America 2020:
   A National Mental Health Crisis," APA.org, October 2020,
   https://www.apa.org/news/press/releases/stress/2020/sia-mental
   -health-crisis.pdf.

5. Chris Melore, "Mighty Moms: 3 in 4 Millennial Mothers
   Are Hiding Their Stress from Their Families,"
   StudyFinds.org, May 20, 2022, https://studyfinds.org
   /millennial-moms-stress-families.

6. Scott Edwards, "Love and the Brain," *On the Brain*, Spring 2015,
   Harvard Medical School, https://hms.harvard.edu/news-events
   /publications-archive/brain/love-brain.

7. Randi Gunther, "How Love Can Conquer Fear," *Psychology
   Today*, March 27, 2020, https://www.psychologytoday.com/us
   /blog/rediscovering-love/202003/how-love-can-conquer-fear.

CHAPTER 5

1. St. Augustine, *Confessions*, trans. Henry Chadwick, Oxford's
   World Classics (Oxford University Press, 1991), book one,
   section i.

CHAPTER 7

1. Daniel G. Amen, *Change Your Brain, Change Your Life (Revised
   and Expanded): The Breakthrough Program for Conquering
   Anxiety, Depression, Obsessiveness, Lack of Focus, Anger, and
   Memory Problems* (Harmony Books, 2015).

2. Denise Winterman, "Rumination: The Danger of Dwelling," *BBC
   News Magazine*, October 17, 2013, https://www.bbc.com/news
   /magazine-24444431.

CHAPTER 8

1. A. W. Tozer, *The Purpose of Man: Designed to Worship*, ed. James L. Snyder (Bethany House, 2009), 184.
2. Juliana Sabatello, "Co-Regulation: How Just Being with Someone Can Help," HealthyPlace.com, September 13, 2021, https://www .healthyplace.com/blogs/relationshipsandmentalillness/2021/9 /co-regulation-how-just-being-with-someone-can-help.

CHAPTER 9

1. Barbara Kerr, s.v. "creativity," *Encyclopedia Britannica*, last updated July 2, 2024, https://www.britannica.com/topic /creativity.
2. Amy F. T. Arnsten, "Stress Signalling Pathways That Impair Prefrontal Cortex Structure and Function," *Nature Reviews Neuroscience* 10 (June 2009): 410–22, https://www.nature.com /articles/nrn2648.
3. Harvard Medical School, "Protect Your Brain from Stress," Harvard Health Publishing, February 15, 2021, https://www.health.harvard.edu/mind-and-mood /protect-your-brain-from-stress.

ABOUT THE AUTHOR

BECKY THOMPSON IS A *USA TODAY* BESTSELLING AUTHOR AND THE CREATOR of the Midnight Mom Devotional online community, where over two million moms gather in nightly prayer. She is the author of the books *Hope Unfolding, Love Unending, Truth Unchanging, My Real Story, Peace,* and *God So Close.* She coauthored the *Midnight Mom Devotional* and *Tonight We Pray for the Momma* with her mom, Susan K. Pitts, and *Midnight Dad Devotional* with her dad, Dr. Mark Pitts. Becky currently lives in Northwest Oklahoma with her husband, Jared, and their three children, Kolton, Kadence, and Jaxton.

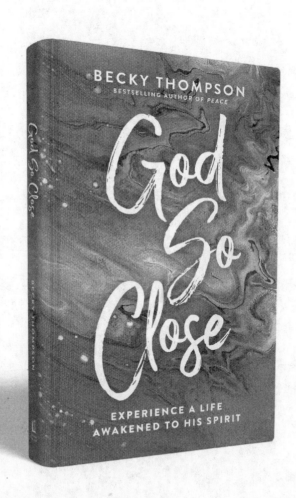

From the Publisher

GREAT BOOKS

ARE EVEN BETTER WHEN THEY'RE SHARED!

Help other readers find this one:

- Post a review at your favorite online bookseller

- Post a picture on a social media account and share why you enjoyed it

- Send a note to a friend who would also love it—or better yet, give them a copy

Thanks for reading!